the SECRETS FILE

D1630748

'A popular government, without popular information or the means of acquiring it, is but a prologue to a farce or a tragedy; or, perhaps both. Knowledge will forever govern ignorance; and a people who mean to be their own governors must arm themselves with the power which knowledge gives.'

James Madison
President of the United States of America, 1822

the SECRETS FILE

THE CASE FOR FREEDOM OF INFORMATION IN BRITAIN TODAY

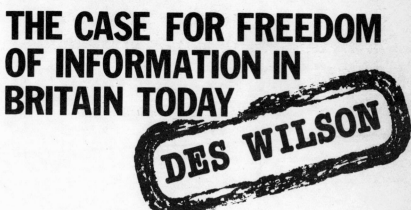

DES WILSON

Foreword by
The Rt. Hon. David Steel MP

Heinemann Educational Books
London · Portsmouth (New Hampshire)

Heinemann Educational Books Ltd
22 Bedford Square, London WC1B 3HH

Heinemann Educational Books Inc
70 Court Street, Portsmouth, New Hampshire 03801

ISBN 0 435 83940 3
ISBN 0 435 83939 X Pbk

First published 1984

Typeset and printed in Great Britain by
Biddles Ltd, Guildford, Surrey

CONTENTS

EDITORS NOTES AND ACKNOWLEDGEMENTS

I thank my colleague, Maurice Frankel, for his considerable assistance with this book, and also the other contributors, Ron Bailey and James Michael.

A number of books were particularly helpful and they are listed on page 159. I thank all those who permitted extracts from their work to be published in this book.

My colleagues Susan Dibb and Patricia Simms have, as always, been most supportive.

The 1984 Campaign for Freedom of Information was launched in January 1984. One of its tactics has been to publish a series of 'Secrets Files' and Chapters 3–5 are based on three of these. Chapter 5 draws, with thanks, on contributions to a Secrets File by the Advisory Centre for Education, the Childrens Legal Centre, the Community Rights Project, MIND, the National Association for Young People in Care, the National Council for Civil Liberties, Patients Association, and Reform University Laws and Educational Standards. The Campaign's work will continue beyond 1984 and I hope this book will prove an invaluable handbook for the campaign as well as rewarding to all its readers.

Des Wilson, September 1984

NOTES ON CONTRIBUTORS

DES WILSON is, at the time of publication, Chairman of the Campaign for Freedom of Information in Britain, and also Chairman of Friends of the Earth, and of CLEAR, The Campaign for Lead-free Air. Born in New Zealand, he came to Britain in 1960 and was the first Director of Shelter, the National Campaign for the Homeless (1966–71). He has been active in other pressure groups, and in the Liberal party, and is also a well-known journalist, having been a columnist on both *The Guardian* and *The Observer*, editor of *Social Work Today* from 1976 to 1979, and Deputy Editor of the *Illustrated London News* from 1979 to 1981. His other books for Heinemann Educational Books are *The Lead Scandal: The Fight to Save Children from the Damage from Lead in Petrol* (1983), *The Environmental Crisis: A Handbook for all Friends of the Earth* (1984), and *Pressure: The A–Z of Campaigning in Britain* (1984).

MAURICE FRANKEL is a full-time campaigner with the 1984 Campaign for Freedom of Information and an environmental pollution consultant for Friends of the Earth. After graduating in biology he worked for a number of years with Social Audit. He is the author of *The Alkali Inspectorate: the Control of Industrial Air Pollution* (1974), *The Social Audit Pollution Handbook* (1978), *A Word of Warning: the Quality of Chemical Suppliers' Health & Safety Information* (1981), and *Chemical Risk: A Workers' Guide to Chemical Hazards and Data Sheets* (1982).

RON BAILEY is the local government co-ordinator of the Community Rights Project, an organisation which campaigns for greater public access rights and consultation by local authorities and health authorities. He is also involved in other projects to ensure that local authorities carry out their duties. He had just completed a new book entitled *Influencing Town Hall Policy: A Guide to Your Rights*, which is due to be published in 1984 by Penguin Books. He has also for many years been a dedicated campaigner for the homeless.

JAMES MICHAEL was educated in the United States and admitted to the District of Columbia Bar. He worked as an editor with US Law Week, was staff counsel with the National Commission on Product Safety, and a member of Ralph Nader's Center for Study of Responsive Law. He moved to London in 1972 and has a LL.M. from the London School of Economics. He is now Senior Lecturer in Law at the Polytechnic of Central London. He is an acknowledged authority on worldwide initiatives towards greater freedom of information.

FOREWORD BY THE Rt. Hon. DAVID STEEL MP

[handwritten notes: Policy making- Individual Rights- Accountability- End official Secrets act → FOIA (see next page)]

Two clear messages emerge from this book: first, that the level of secrecy in Britain today has reached proportions that seriously undermine the health of our democracy; second, that this is a cause that should have the support of all who are concerned with the quality of that democracy, no matter which political party they support, or what their level of involvement in public life. The authors demonstrate convincingly that secrecy leads to poor policy-making and to considerable injustice to individuals.

Politicians of all parties have paid lip-service to freedom of information in opposition, but failed to act when in office. The reason for this is obvious; information is power. In a country where power has become too centralised, and whose bureaucracies are no longer properly accountable to the people, freedom of information is, in the words of one former civil servant, 'not a fashionable option but a precondition for any serious attempt to solve the country's underlying problems'. We need a wider input of knowledge and expertise into decision-making. Decision-makers should be constantly in receipt of advice and information, not only from the professionals and public servants, but from all sections of the community and from individual citizens. Proper public participation, however, is impossible unless information is more widely shared.

There are other reasons why freedom of information is of real importance. One is to protect the rights of the individual. It is really extraordinary that so many files could now be kept on individual citizens without their having right of access to them, and thus the opportunity to check that they are correct and fair. Individual files are accessible to many people – there is no reason why, with sensible exemptions, they should not be equally accessible to the people most directly concerned.

Above all, we need to keep our local and national civil services fully accountable. This will increase their competence and efficiency. The principle of responsibility – to the electorate and parliament – needs to be maintained and strengthened and it cannot be done when our governmental system is bedevilled by secrecy.

When the Australians considered freedom of information, their Senate Standing Committee stated: 'The essence of democracy lies in the ability of people to make choices: about who shall govern; or about which policies they support or reject. Such choices cannot be properly made unless adequate information is available. It cannot be accepted that it is the government itself which has determined what level of information is to be regarded as adequate.' That is why the authors, and the 1984 Campaign for Freedom of Information, are correct to argue that a system of greater voluntary disclosure will not work.

We need a full Freedom of Information Act in Britain, just as we need to repeal the totally unacceptable Official Secrets Act and replace it with a much narrower version dealing only with national security. That is why this year I took advantage of the ten-minute rule procedure to introduce a Bill myself with all-party support.

The detail of the case I leave to the authors; I return finally, to the issue of democracy itself. A genuine democracy extends far beyond the right of citizens to have the occasional vote for their Member of Parliament or local councillor. The real test is whether people can influence decisions as they are taken, can know exactly what is happening and why, and, ideally, find it possible to support decisions and policies on the basis of access to the facts.

I am pleased to say that the Liberal Party has been a firm supporter of freedom of information for many years, and the last major attempt to introduce such legislation into the House of Commons was by my colleague Clement Freud whose Bill fell with the end of the Labour Government in May 1979.

I have been pleased to note that the leaders of both the Labour and Social Democratic Parties have firmly committed themselves to support legislation as well, and also that a number of leading Conservatives have made clear their view that the time has come for action. If ever there was an issue that should be an all-party issue, and if ever there was an issue that should be decided by the people, and by ordinary councillors and back-benchers, it is this one, for it is about control of those who hold the reins of power, and one can never expect objective decisions to relinquish power to be taken by them.

Des Wilson and his colleagues claim that a more open approach will reinforce the qualities of honesty and integrity in public life, and this view I share. It is extraordinary that they need to devote so much energy to fight for freedom of information, for it should be the secretive who are forced to argue and defend their position. It is extraordinary, too, that the really secretive will not even come out into the open to argue their corner. Perhaps this is not really surprising, however, for as Milton wrote, 'Whoever saw truth put to flight in free and open encounter?'

PART 1 SECRECY IN BRITAIN

1 1984.... AND ONWARDS? THE LEVEL AND EFFECTS OF SECRECY IN BRITAIN TODAY

DES WILSON

Of all democratic countries in the world today, i.e. those that are not dictatorships or subject to one-party rule, Britain is probably the most secretive. Undoubtedly its secrecy is more institutionalised than in any comparable country, but equally important, the habit of, and instinct for, secrecy, are more entrenched in the psyche of the governing and managerial elite than is the case in any comparable country.

Governmental secrecy is institutionalised by the Official Secrets Act. Section 2 of this Act, in the words of the 1972 report of a Committee of Inquiry under Lord Franks, 'catches all official documents and information. It makes no distinction of kind, and no distinctions of degree. All information which a crown servant learns in the course of his duty is "official" for the purposes of Section 2, whatever its nature, whatever its importance, whatever its original source. A blanket is thrown over everything; nothing escapes.'

In addition to the Official Secrets Act there are over 100 statutes making the disclosure of information by civil servants or others a criminal office. As well as the legislation, there are civil service rules and a civil service classification system based on an implicit assumption that virtually all documents fall within one of four classifications: Top Secret, Secret, Confidential, or Restricted.

Reinforced by these laws and regulations, secrecy has become a disease that has spread from Whitehall to envelop local authorities as well as national authorities, other statutory bodies and quangos, nationalised industries and private commerce. It is a disease that has its roots in the cynical practice of power (see Chapter 2) and that under-mines the health of our democracy. It is a disease that has been diagnosed by many influential individuals and committees of inquiry in the past.

In 1968 the Committee on the Civil Service, chaired by Lord Fulton, reported that 'the administrative process is surrounded by too much secrecy. The public interest would be better served if there were a greater amount of openness.'

In 1972 the Franks Committe reported of the Official Secrets Act that 'Its scope is enormously wide. Any law which impinges on the freedom of information in a democracy should be much more tightly drawn.'

In 1977 the Royal Commission on the Press reported that 'The right of access to information which is of legitimate concern to people, Parliament and press is too restricted and this, combined with the general secrecy with which government is conducted, has caused much injustice, some corruption, and many mistakes.'

In 1979 a government Green Paper admitted that 'Administration is still conducted in an atmosphere of secrecy which cannot always be justified.' It stated that the 'catch-all effect of Section 2 of the Official Secrets Act is no longer right.'

In later chapters we will see how, despite the advice of the above official reports, the Official Secrets Act remains, and freedom of infor-mation legislation is refused; we will look at why this is so, and what effects it has on individuals and community life. This chapter, however, concentrates on the extent and nature of secrecy in Britain today, and it is accompanied in Part 2 by three extensive 'files' on secrecy: Maurice Frankel describes how it obstructs the path to adequate environmental protection and helps the polluter; also how it perpetuates inaccuracy and often injustice in individual files; and Ron Bailey demonstrates how freedom of information varies considerably from Town Hall to Town Hall and how secretive many local authorities still are.

The price we pay for secrecy cannot be over-stated. The imbalance of access to information between governors and governed in Britain is of such size and scope that it seriously undermines the health of our democracy.

- The sources of power and influence are obscured.
- Public servants are not properly accountable.
- Public participation is seriously hampered.
- Justice is often not seen to be done.
- Inefficiency and error are made more likely.

Let's take this last point first. One of the most devastating critiques of overspending and waste in Whitehall is contained in Leslie Chapman's book, *Your Disobedient Servant*. Chapman, who joined the civil service at 20 and was a regional director with the Ministry of Works when he retired in 1973 at the age of 53, complained of 'massive waste of taxpayers' money and repeated failures to carry out instructions given by Ministers'. In his book he argues with plenty of evidence that secrecy costs the taxpayer a fortune. 'There can be no shadow of doubt', he writes, 'that the Official Secrets Act, as it is at present worded and used, contributes to the continuance of waste and extravagance on a massive scale in the public sector, and protects those who are responsible from the consequences of inefficiency, error and downright negligence.'

And elsewhere: 'This book is concerned only with the financial consequences of unnecessary secrecy in the public sector and there should be no room for misunderstanding on this point: while the Official Secrets Act is used as it is in this country, bungling and incompetence of all kinds can flourish undetected and the taxpayer will pay dearly for this. . . . As soon as the restrictions are lifted many of the events which now give rise to complaint will not happen'.

In *The Civil Servants* Peter Kellner and Lord Crowther-Hunt tell the story of *Concorde*:

In the 1960s when the important decisions were being taken, there was no effective opportunity to challenge publicly the false optimism about its prospects. And because there were no adequate outside checks the internal system of checks and balances – with the Treasury supposed to act as a questioning foil to departmental enthusiasm – was allowed to fail unnoticed. Professor David Henderson, Chief Economist at the Ministry of Aviation from 1965–67 recently said: 'Even now we don't know whose opinions counted at what stage, what figures were accepted on what evidence at what stage, what outside checks were made. How can one justify that? How can we pretend to be trying to learn lessons from experience?' Henderson was asked whether outside, independent checks were ever made on the economics of Concorde: 'Not that I am aware of. . . . It offends the British adminstrator's sense of what is orderly.

In 1982, it was estimated that the cost of pulling down and replacing thousands of faulty system-built homes put up during the 1960s and 1970s could run into thousands of millions, yet the problem could have been averted in 1969 when a secret report identified fundamental flaws in the new building system. The report was commissioned from the government's National Building Association by the London Borough of Hillingdon after it had found water leaking into brand new estates built using the new systems. The report was never published and the government continued to urge local authorities to use the flawed systems. In 1982, it was estimated that the costs of dealing with the defective homes throughout the country could be as high as £3,000 million (*Sunday Times*, 18 April 1982).

In order to look at the extent of secrecy, we should divide it into two areas:

First, secrecy in policy decision-making, affecting the community as a whole.

Second, secrecy directly affecting the individual.

Secrecy in policy making

Secrecy is the enemy of rational decision making – and the friend of political prejudice. It allows governments to cover up errors, suppress dissenting views, and conceal the fact that their policies may not be working or may even be having the opposite effects to those intended.

The press report below strikingly illustrates the way in which Ministers may first suppress and then rewrite reports that may not support their political philosophy:

A Whitehall report which was withheld from the public on the specific instructions of Mr Nigel Lawson, the Energy Secretary, flatly contradicts the Government's claim that there is no case for devoting more resources to energy conservation.

The report was drawn up by the Department of Energy's policy unit in response to the Commons energy committee's criticism that Whitehall had no clear idea of whether investing about £1,300 million in a new nuclear power station was as cost effective as spending a similar amount to promote energy conservation.

Its conclusions are so unpalatable to the Government that it has not been published. Instead . . . the Department published another report under Mr Lawson's close supervision.

The report . . . is sceptical about the value of any further role by the Government in energy conservation.

The Government last year implicitly denied the existence of the first report . . .

The Department's published report says that because of all the uncertainties 'it is difficult to find an economic justification for direct Government involvement in fuel use choices made by consumers'.

But according to the unpublished report 'there are significant and continuing national benefits to be gained from increased conservation investment'.

In its published document the Department says that there must be 'a presupposition that there is no Public-Sector Borrowing Requirement advantage in bringing forward conservation'. Yet according to the unpublished study: 'in the longer term, increased conservation investment should reduce the call on public funds for energy supply'.

(*The Guardian*, 3 March 1983)

Government blunders are most easily concealed in the field of defence, where secrecy can be justified by claims that 'national security' is at risk. Chapman Pincher, in his book *Inside Story* describes how Ministry of Defence officials refused to provide a select committee on expenditure with information about the costs of the proposed Poseidon missile system. 'The Defence Ministry officials refused to supply cost estimates on security grounds though full details of the dollar costs had been published in the USA.' The real reason for the secrecy was that 'the navy planners had made a monumental mistake when preparing their estimates for securing Poseidon, on which they were immensely keen. They had given an estimate of £250 million, but discussions with the Pentagon, which had already deployed the weapon, showed that the true cost would prove to be almost double that figure'.

Exactly how policy decisions are reached in Whitehall is difficult to describe, partly because of secrecy itself, and partly because the process differs between Ministries and between issues. However, there is usually some consultation with what the Ministry believes to be interested parties. These are often the financial vested interests, and the element of public consultation can be slight. At present the submissions by vested interests remain secret. It is thus impossible for outsiders to gauge the influence that vested interests have had, or independently to assess the quality of their submissions. The balance of the information and arguments submitted to government, and the accuracy of it, would be considerably improved if it was known they were to be published. (Exemptions could still be maintained for those items of information that would genuinely assist competitors of the industries concerned.)

Usually the detailed arguments, facts and figures, upon which policy decisions are eventually taken, are exchanged between Ministries and civil servants, but are not published. It is thus impossible for opposition politicians, outside organisations or the public to compare the ministerial decision with the arguments, facts and figures presented on the issue in order to test the consistency of the decision against the evidence produced. Here, too, it is arguable that if the background papers containing the arguments, facts and figures were open to wider inspection, they might be improved, and it would be less likely that political bias would enter into the final decisions.

The problem with the present secretive way in which policy debate takes places is that there is the minimum of input, and the wider public debate usually takes place only after the decision is announced. Once they have committed themselves to a decision, Ministers feel bound to defend it, and are unlikely to change their minds. The debate itself, therefore, is unreal. The right time for public debate is *before* decisions are taken, when Ministers can still change their minds without loss of face, and when the maximum public participation in the decision-making process can be realised.

A former civil servant, William Plowden, speaking on television in 1978, indicated what can happen when policy discussions take place behind the Whitehall 'wall':

> They develop like any kind of closed profession, a culture and a language of their own. They communicate with each other in terms that they understand; phrases like 'at the end of the day', 'ball's in your court', a 'sticky wicket' are largely used inside the civil service. And I think the sorts of arguments they use are phrased in terms which they recognise and which convey their meaning to each other, but which wouldn't carry so much conviction with an outside audience. . . . The thing about the language of Whitehall is that it makes it unnecessary very often to carry arguments right through to the end, because so many assumptions are shared. It is not so much the language as the culture really. So many assumptions are shared that one doesn't need to argue every point out in detail in the way you would if you were trying to persuade a hostile or certainly critical outside audience.

Undoubtedly this is an area of real concern: that secrecy covers up poor policy-making, the lack of a well-argued case, the restriction on the consideration of alternative options, and the predomination of established biases within decision-making circles.

If Britain's record over the past thirty or forty years had been one of brilliant decision-making and progress or was at least comparable with those of similar countries, it might be argued that the system works. But the record of poor decision-making and poor performance across the whole economic, environmental and social front suggests a need to broaden the base of factual and intellectual input, and that can only be possible in circumstances where information is more widely shared and government takes place much more in the open.

Secrecy affecting the individual

With so many controls now imposed by the State, and so many decisions taken at State level, and given the unprecedented technology that exists to collect and record information, there has never been a more urgent need than exists today for the balance between the rights of the individual and the community to be carefully weighed, and for the careful surveillance by the people of the use of State power.

In one respect there is an unacceptable imbalance; it occurs because files are kept on individual members of the public by public servants and 'professionals', but access to those files is reserved for the public servants and 'professionals' alone. Not only does the individual not know what is in his or her file, but he or she does not know how many people have seen that file and in what circumstances, or what decisions they have taken on the basis of what information.

The main argument of the professionals is that, somehow, all this is 'in our own interests'. They say that patients may be upset, and their health problems made more serious, if they discover the truth about their illnesses. Families could be disturbed by the frank comments on their children by school teachers. So-called 'clients' of the social services could be caused distress by having the realities of their lives stated frankly on paper. At its best, this argument is paternalistic. It assumes that adults do not want to, or cannot, face the facts about their own lives. It is an unwarranted assumption. The truth is that it is a cover up for the real reason why professionals wish to deny the public the right to their own files – namely, they wish to preserve the exclusivity and the mystique that are both necessary for their self-esteem and protect them from their own mistakes or misjudgements.

Of course, some patients may not wish to know all their medical details; in that case, they do not have to ask for the file. Also there may be grounds for denial of access to files in exceptional circumstances, such as where somebody's life could be in danger. Many others may feel no need to look at their files anyway – life may be proceeding smoothly and they may have no motivation to bother. There is, however, an over-riding reason why the individual *must* have the right of access if he or she desires it, and that is the extremely high possibility of error. The number of personal files is massive and the scope for inaccuracy and injustice is so considerable that it has to be assumed that these must occur on a daily basis. There is simply no guarantee whether file entries are fact or fiction. The case for our automatic right of access to files about ourselves is so overwhelming that it is as much a tribute to our own docility as it is to the arrogance of the system that we have not demanded and obtained it before.

At present, parents are held responsible in law for the education of their children, but have no right of access to their children's school files. Social workers maintain extensive files on their so-called 'clients', but the clients have no right of access to those files. Patients have no right of access to their own medical records. Tenants of local authority housing, or those on local authority waiting lists, cannot check their files to see that they are accurate.

It really is an extraordinary state of affairs when people who, at the end of the day, are the servants of the individual, can deny the individual crucial facts about his or her own life. The serious concern is that crucial decisions can be taken on incorrect facts, and then it can be almost impossible for the subject of the file to understand what has happened.

In Chapter 5, Maurice Frankel pulls together contributions from a number of organisations concerned about this matter. Their stories and case histories show that the refusal to allow individuals access to their files is one of the most unacceptable aspects of secrecy in Britain today.

Maurice Frankel also looks at the risks to the individual caused by environmental secrecy (Chapter 3). His report demonstrates that the path to adequate environmental protection in Britain is blocked by an unacceptable level of secrecy demanded by industry and supported by the governmental agencies. Because of this, an uncertain public is unable to obtain the information it needs on:

●   what the hazards are;
●   where the hazards are;
●   whether safety limits required by law are being observed.

The secrecy has many different causes and is explained and justified in many different ways; in some cases it is imposed by law and in others it is the result of deals between industry and the authorities. Taken in its totality, it is a national scandal:

●   The location of some 2,000 major hazard sites (involving the use of dangerous chemicals) is officially secret as a result of pressure from industry.

●   The Industrial Air Pollution Inspectorate is prohibited by law from revealing details of the pollution released by the factories it regulates.

●   While the Health and Safety At Work Act requires that employees be given information about hazards at work, people who live alongside the factories and could be exposed to the same hazards are denied that information. An inspector who reveals it may be in breach of the law.

●   The pesticides industry operates behind a blanket of almost total security, helped by the Advisory Committee on Pesticides which refuses to disclose information about the hazards of pesticides it clears for use. The ACP has refused to identify products now known to have been cleared as safe on the basis of invalid research.

●   Measures proposed in the 1974 Control of Pollution Act to make more information available about industrial pollution of rivers have been repeatedly delayed and are still not in force ten years later.

●   Industry demands widespread secrecy supposedly to protect trade secrets, but in many cases there are no valid commercial reasons for withholding the information.

Shortly after the 1984 Campaign published the results of this research, the Tenth Report of the Royal Commission on Environmental Pollution was published. It reinforced our complaint, and its Chairman, Professor Sir Richard Southwood, when questioned on television that evening, stated that secrecy was the number one obstacle to better environmental protection.

Once more, one of the official defences for secrecy is that the public can't handle the facts. There would be unnecessary panic. In fact, concern and panic are far more likely to be aroused by secrecy, and the fear that we are not being told the truth, than by secrecy of the kind that implies that someone has something to hide.

In some parts of Britain, notably in Yorkshire, there is much controversy over the fact that water authorities meet in secret. Water authorities were first set up in the early seventies and were subject to the Public Bodies (Admission to Meetings) Act 1960, guaranteeing their meetings would be open to the press and public. However, in 1983 a Water Act designed to 'reduce bureaucracy' came into force. It cut the size of Boards, in particular by eliminating the large number of local authority representatives, and took away right of access of the public and the press.

Water authorities now meet in secret. The defence was that the water authorities were moving over to an executive style of operation. Lord Bellwin explained to the House of Lords, 'The new small executive boards of the water authorities will be totally different in character. . . . It is impossible to function effectively as a member of such a board if at every stage one is concerned that the odd word here, the odd outspoken comment there, will hit the headlines the next day.'

He added, 'The presence of outsiders at meetings of this kind has a profoundly inhibiting effect on discussion. People will not speak up as freely as they would in private. To deny that is simply to turn one's back on reality.' This had, of course, applied to the old water authorities and they dealt with the problem by going into private session whenever they needed to.

Water authorities spend vast sums of public money, and have powers of taxation, i.e. water rates. Their business also has considerable importance for local communities. Not only are they responsible for building reservoirs or sewage works, but also their responsibilities relate to public health, safety and amenity. Now, most of these matters will be dealt with in secret; the water authorities are effectively not accountable.

Of course, the water authorities don't have to close their meetings to press and the public. However, the nine English authorities have, without exception, voted for secrecy. Only the Welsh water authority decided to continue to meet in public. Its public information officer argued, in a paper circulated to members, that the authority would benefit from a well-informed press with full access to official papers. 'It is fair to assert that any stemming of the flow of knowledge can only result in an ill-informed, suspicious and therefore critical news coverage of all aspects of the authority's work', he argued.

Other nationalised industries are also highly secretive. British Gas, for instance, monitors, but does not disclose, the levels of defects found in new gas appliances. It also has target standards of service to domestic consumers but does not publicly reveal what these are, or how often they are achieved. In answer to one query, Sir Denis Rooke, Chairman of the British Gas Corporation, wrote, 'I would point out that the

Corporation, while a statutory corporation, is not expending public money in the normally accepted sense of that term and that no special onus for disclosure arises on that account.'

The London Electricity Consultative Council, a statutory consumer body, reported in 1983 that the Electricity Council 'had consistently withheld the data from its market surveys of consumer satisfaction and in 1982 declined to publicly account for the loss of £80 million by the industry's pension fund, the burden of it carried by the consumer'. It added that the London Electricity Board had rejected its suggestions that papers and minutes about non-confidential matters discussed at Board meetings should be deposited in public libraries. The LECC estimated that only about 20 per cent of the items discussed at these meetings were genuinely confidential.

Ron Bailey in Chapter 4 addresses Town Hall secrecy. It can sometimes be absurd. In December 1983 the London Borough of Barking and Dagenham's carnival committee went into secret session at the end of their meeting: 'It was resolved to exclude the public from the remainder of the meeting in view of the confidential nature of the business.' It then decided in secret session, 'We do not feel able to accede to a request made by the local Chamber of Trade and Commerce to borrow the carnival bunting to decorate the town centre for Christmas as we do not feel it to be an appropriate type of decoration for use over the Christmas period.'

Later the same month its cleansing committee 'resolved to exclude the public from the remainder of the meeting by reason of the confidential nature of the business to be transacted' and after the secret discussion concluded: 'We have acceded to a request from the Community Programme Division for a free supply of 25 refuse sacks per week for a period of one year to assist the charity work carried out by the division.'

Secrecy also affects the consumer in the High Street. Using the consumer's money as taxpayer, Whitehall monitors a wide range of consumer goods and services. It does this partly because it is a prolific buyer of many products, from cars to stationery. It therefore has become an expert on comparable quality and cost of products. Much of this information is kept secret. Yet, in the United States it is possible to have access to this data. The National Consumer Council's report 'Consuming Secrets' spells this out in detail. For instance, 'The Department of Transport has been collecting and publishing statistics on failure rates of passenger vehicles since 1968, but details of which cars have been found to have which faults have never been published, valuable though this information would be to prospective car buyers. Although the aggregate information – for example, 21 per cent of cars failed the test in 1978 because of brake defects – is interesting, the question of which specific makes of cars failed the tests is more than merely interesting; it could be a matter of life and death.'

There are, of course, many other areas where excessive secrecy affects the public directly – in planning, in transport, and in energy, to name just three. Those who suffer most from secrecy, however, tend to be those who are most vulnerable anyway. For instance, if the public does not know of an injustice it can be easily perpetuated and resources required to deal with it are not produced. A case in point is provision for the mentally handicapped. In 1983 *The Guardian* published details of reports covering 50 hospitals and 30 homes for the mentally handicapped, revealing widespread instances of overcrowding, under-staffing, custodial attitudes to patients, fire risks and the denial of basic human dignity. The details were contained in reports that were confidential. The researchers had been made to sign the Official Secrets Act before they could even visit the hospitals. The mentally handi-capped, closeted in these hospitals and homes, are particularly vulnerable to neglect unless the public are kept aware of their existence and their problems. The fact that these enquiries and reports were secret protected the authorities from criticism and pressure to act. As a result of *The Guardian's* campaign on the issue, however, it is now possible that reports will be published.

One of the ironies of secrecy in Britain is that it is possible to obtain information in Washington by using the United States Freedom of Information Act which is confidential in Britain. For instance, Friends of the Earth opposing the plans to build a pressurised water reactor (PWR) at Sizewell used the Act to uncover research by the UK Atomic Energy Authority into the safety of the PWR that was secret in Britain but available in Washington.

The report assessed work carried out at the American Oakridge Laboratories into the risk of severe damage to the core of the PWR. It was based on actual incidents at American nuclear power plants. The work indicated that the chances of a melt-down could be between 1 in 200 and 1 in 600 reactor years. This is much higher than the 1 in 20,000 reactor years previously predicted. The UK Atomic Energy Authority largely endorsed the Oakridge figures.

The US Food and Drug Administration (FDA) will release copies of the reports produced by their inspectors visiting British toxicology laboratories: these must meet FDA standards before their results can be submitted to the agency.

To fully appreciate the extent to which the individual is denied infor-mation affecting his or her life, let's take the case of a not unusual family – mother and father and two children of school age, living in a council house, say Mr and Mrs Smith and their children, Ben and Nat.

- The Smiths are not allowed to see the school files on Ben and Nat.

- The Smiths are not allowed to see any of their family's medical records.

- The Smiths cannot go to the Town Hall and see their file in the housing office, nor can they go to the social services office and see a file on them that exists there.

- They have been recipients of welfare benefits, but they are not allowed to see their social security file.

- Like all members of the public, they cannot attend sub-committee meetings of their local council, nor are their local newspapers allowed to report them.

- They cannot attend meetings of their local water authority, nor can they find reports of them in their local newspaper.

- They live near a big factory handling chemicals, and Mr Smith, as an employee, is entitled under the Health and Safety at Work Act to be told of the potential hazards and safeguards. However, he is not allowed to tell Mrs Smith because this information is restricted to employees only.

- The Smiths have been refused a mortgage by two building societies but have been given no reason why. They cannot see their file to see if the building societies have based their decision on accurate information.

- The Smiths have had some difficulty with their insurance company, and are convinced that the insurance company is acting on the basis of incorrect records, but are not allowed to see their file to check what it says.

- Mr Smith is very concerned about the location of sites in England for the disposal of radioactive waste, believing that one is planned for his own locality. His Member of Parliament raised the question in the House of Commons but was told that 'the sites are not comprehensively listed' (i.e. are not named).

- Mr Smith is a keen cyclist and wrote to the Ministry of Transport to ask for a report he knew existed on options for better cycle safety. He is told this is 'a restricted document' (this actually happened to a member of Friends of the Earth).

Sitting before their gas fire one night, Mr and Mrs Smith considered all these facts, and came to the conclusion that they lived in a highly secretive society. At that moment the gas fire exploded and considerable damage was caused.

Months afterwards, the Smiths still had no idea what caused the explosion. The Gas Board informed them that their report on the incident was confidential!

2 INFORMATION IS POWER: THE CAUSES OF SECRECY

DES WILSON

To begin this chapter with Section 2 of the Official Secrets Act is not to say that it is the cause of secrecy in Britain. It is not; nor are the 100-odd statutes with non-disclosure clauses, or the civil service instructions on classification of documents. All this is the *machinery of secrecy* – the means whereby those who have the information either keep it to themselves or control its release. The rules and regulations institutionalise secrecy, but the real cause is the desire for secrecy of those in power.

That said, there is no question that the Official Secrets Act plus the other legislation and administrative controls deeply affect the attitudes and behaviour of all within our bureaucracies. The machinery works. I shall, therefore, deal with these secondary factors, with the machinery of secrecy, first.

The infamous Section 2

As a basis for control and cover-up, Section 2 of the Official Secrets Act would be as satisfactory to a one-party communist state or the most oppressive of dictatorships as it is to its defenders in Britain. It was enacted in extraordinary circumstances in 1911 when war seemed imminent. Presented to the House of Commons as an emergency action, it achieved all its readings and the committee stage in thirty minutes. The extraordinary atmosphere in the House is described by the then Under Secretary of State for War, Major-General J. E. B. Seeley:

I got up and proposed that the Bill should be read a second time, explaining, in two sentences only, that it was considered desirable in the public interest that the measure should be passed. Hardly a word was said and the Bill was read a second time; the Speaker left the Chair. I then moved the Bill in Committee. This was the first critical moment; two men got up to speak, but both were forcibly pulled down by their neighbours after they had uttered a few sentences, and the Committee stage was passed. The Speaker walked back to his chair and said: 'The question is, that I report this Bill without amendment to the House'. Again two or three people stood up; again they were pulled down by their neighbours, and the report stage was through. The Speaker turned to me and said: 'The third reading, what day?'. 'Now, sir', I replied. My heart beat fast as the Speaker said: 'The question is that this Bill be read a third time'. It was open to anyone of the members of the House of Commons to get up and say that no bill had ever yet been passed through all its stages in one day without a word of explanation from the minister in charge. . . . But to the eternal honour of those members, to whom I now offer, on behalf of that and all succeeding governments, my most grateful thanks, not one man seriously opposed, and in a little more time than it has taken to write these words that formidable piece of legislation was passed.

Thus was enacted a piece of legislation that was described by Professor H. W. R. Wade, QC, Professor of English Law at the University of Oxford, in evidence to the Franks Committee in 1971, as 'a blot on the statute book which needs to be removed . . . so crude, and so excessively severe, that it is rendered tolerable in practice only by . . . tight control of prosecutions'.

The Franks Committee appeared to share this view:

We found Section 2 a mess. Its scope is enormously wide. Any law which impinges on the freedom of information in a democracy should be much more tightly drawn. A catch-all provision is saved from absurdity in operation only by the sparing exercise of the Attorney-General's discretion to prosecute.

The section specifies several other situations in which other persons are also caught:

a Government contractors and their employees are treated in the same way as Crown servants. Information which they learn in that capacity counts as 'official' for the purposes of the section, and the unauthorised disclosure of such information is an offence. The nature of the information is irrelevant.

b Any person to whom official information is entrusted in confidence by a Crown servant is prohibited from making any unauthorised disclosure of that information.

c Any person in possession of official information 'which has been made or obtained in contravention' of the Official Secrets Act is prohibited from making it possible to have a 'chain' of unauthorised communications, with each link in the chain committing an offence by passing on the information. In effect, the unauthorised handling of official information is an offence in much the same way as handling stolen goods is an offence.

Nor does Section 2 stop there. Not only does it make it an offence to disclose official information, but it also makes it an offence to receive it. It has to be proved that the recipient knew at the time of receipt that the information was communicated to him or her in contravention of the Official Secrets Act, and the recipient can defend himself or herself by proving that the information was communicated contrary to his or her desire. But, reports Franks, 'The offence itself under Section 2 consists of simple receipt. It is immaterial whether the recipient subsequently passes on the information or makes any other use of it.'

All those who enter the service of the Crown sign the Official Secrets Act. From that point, they live in an extraordinary world of nods and winks, because, of course, Section 2 is unworkable. If every civil servant took the Act literally, the bureaucracy and society would come to a complete halt. It would mean civil servants could hardly talk or write to each other, let alone anyone else. Ministers, with whom presumably the authority to disclose or to permit disclosure ultimately rests, would spend their entire lives taking decisions about what documents should or should not be made available and to whom.

Fear and restraint

Thus, civil servants need to interpret the *spirit* of the Act in order that they can communicate with the outside world with some efficiency. The more senior they are, the more they can communicate, for the more they are assumed to have discretion. One of the main effects of the Act, therefore, is to reinforce secrecy at the lower levels in the civil service, where men and women don't have the authority or confidence to communicate at their own discretion. Thus there are often absurd inconsistencies, whereby senior civil servants release quite substantial documents or information, whilst totally harmless minor documents are kept secret by civil servants in the lower ranks.

It is often said that the Official Secrets Act is not the fearsome instrument it is supposed to be, because there have been relatively few prosecutions under Section 2. This is more a tribute, however, to the timidity of civil servants and the communal acceptance of secrecy than to the scarcity of prosecutions. The Act remains a substantial controlling influence. When Sir Burke Trend, Secretary of the Cabinet at the time, appeared before the Franks Committee, he talked about the psychological effect of the Act.

He was asked: 'Do you mean on Ministers, senior civil servants, Parliamentary Under-Secretaries – surely not?' He relied: 'On civil servants as a whole, certainly yes I would say that. Do not misunderstand me. I am not saying that you say to yourself "If I say something to X will I be breaching the Official Secrets Act?" *but you are conscious at the back of everything you say and do all day long there is this tremendous sanction.*'

Although, as I have said, the Act is not the fundamental cause of secrecy, because it is the invention and the tool of the secretive, it nevertheless is the number one secondary cause – it is the restraining hand on the shoulder of all civil servants. It is intended to instil fear in both the potential leaker and the potential recipient of information. It is intended to be such a comprehensive protective shield, that almost any form of governmental activity can be obscured. For all their protestations that they are more open than their predecessors, each Party to reach power for over seventy years has retained the Official Secrets Act, and thus made clear that when the chips are down it puts a higher price on secrecy and on control of information than it does on being open.

Civil servants are not only restrained by the Official Secrets Act; they also operate within their own disciplinary procedures, and the documents they sign cover both the Official Secrets Act and these procedures. Within these procedures are a further set of constraints, and civil servants have to become knowledgeable about the different security classifications. These fall under four headings:

> TOP SECRET
> SECRET
> CONFIDENTIAL
> RESTRICTED

As the journalist David Leigh wrote, 'Apart from "unclassified" material, papers are graded (a) hardly secret at all, (b) mildly secret, (c) rather secret, and (d) secret. Or, as Whitehall official puts it, (a) restricted, (b) confidential, (c) secret, and (d) top secret. These words have no objective meaning; one could tune the semantics another way and grade documents (a) secret, (b) very secret, (c) very, very secret, and (d) earth-shatteringly secret.'

The Franks Committee suggested that the internal sanctions linked to these procedures could be of greater practical importance in preventing unauthorised disclosure by civil servants than the Official Secrets Act itself – and these would presumably continue to operate even if Section 2 were repealed. The Committee pointed out that security of employment, and the prospects of promotion, within bureaucracies obsessed with rank and responsibility, are themselves a considerable incentive to conform with secrecy desired by superiors.

Information and power

None of the foregoing explains, however, why the secrecy is necessary, and to whom? The answer is power. Power and information are inextricably linked. This was one of the central themes of George Orwell's 1984. One of the three slogans of 'The Party' in that satire was 'IGNORANCE IS STENGTH'. Put simply, it is the desire of most of those who achieve power to retain that power. To do that they feel a need to create an image of competence, reliability, sound judgement, even of invincibility. As these are extremely difficult standards to meet in our complex world, they rely on a combination of cover-up, public ignorance, manipulation of – sometimes even misrepresentation of – information, and selectivity of disclosure.

This is not the place for a treatise on power, but it is at least this author's view that the concentration of too much power in the hands of too few, too-fallible human beings is a fundamental cause of many of the world's problems today. It is questionable whether even the best of men and women can handle the quantities of power we place in the hands of a few, but unfortunately, the path to power often requires so much compromise, so many sell-outs to principle, so many deals, so many ruthless acts, that those who achieve power are by no means the best of men and women. Even if the best do reach the top, however, it is almost beyond the character of men and women to resist the corruptive influences of power itself. Lord Acton's remark that 'all power corrupts' has been so overwhelmingly substantiated that it must surely be beyond challenge. The only antidotes to the disease are decentralisation and deconcentration of power, and democratic structures of the highest quality. Essential to all of this is freedom of information.

Secrecy helps the powerful

Control of information – secrecy – helps those in power in five main ways. First, *it enables the powerful to maintain a monopoly of power*. The more secretive the centre of power, the more it develops a distance from the people. Lack of information excludes others from participation. In fact, it reduces the desire for participation, because the assumption that those in power have inside knowledge, are in possession of secrets, and are presumably deemed to be the most trustworthy, makes the majority of people feel inadequate and thus admire and respect the powerful. That is, of course, assuming they can recognise the powerful anyway, for secrecy obscures just how powerful the powerful have become.

One defence for the present system is the argument that as Ministers are responsible for their departmental affairs, and accountable directly to Parliament, to whom they have to answer questions, we have an exceptionally open system already. Yet even the Fulton Committee on the Civil Service admitted: 'This assumption is no longer tenable. The Minister and his junior Ministers cannot know all that is going on . . . nor can they nowadays be present at every forum where legitimate questions are raised about departmental activities.'

We know the Prime Minister's power is colossal, but it is even impossible to establish its exact level, for some decisions are taken at Cabinet level, some by the Prime Minister, and some by Cabinet Committees, whose memberships are secret. In fact, the very existence of Cabinet Committees is officially a secret. Exactly where power lies on local authorities varies dramatically from one to another. Beyond the authorities, in local and work institutions, secrecy enables those at the top to develop a mystique, partly based on the fact that they are 'on the inside'. Because it is difficult to challenge those who have all the information, secrecy strengthens the powerful and weakens those who are excluded from the inner circle.

The second benefit the powerful obtain from secrecy is that it stimulates public confidence. The problem with running an organisation openly is that those in power can be more effectively challenged and criticised. If they are inadequate, they can be exposed. The effect, of course, is to reduce their hold on the levers of power. It is hardly surprising, therefore, that from their point of view the control of information is essential. Secrecy covers up mistakes, waste, major policy failures, injustices, and other potential embarrassments. Above all, it covers up *who* is responsible.

Most major organisations, whether national or local authorities, businesses or voluntary agencies, employ 'information officers', except where, with a little more honesty, they are called public relations officers', whose responsibility is not, as their name may imply, to make available information; it is to control information and to present to the public only what the organisation wishes to be known. These people, and they number many thousands, are really involved in the profession of information manipulation, of persuasion and image-creation, of cover up.

'It is no business of any official,' said a Foreign Office witness in the 1970 Official Secrets Trial, 'to allow the government to be embarrassed. That is who we are working for. Embarrassment and security are not really two different things.' Or to put it another way, the creation of public confidence and control of information are 'not really two different things'.

Third, and this is partly linked to the above point, the *control of information is more efficient* from the point of view of the powerful – it leads to more ready acquiescence and enables the powerful to achieve what they want to achieve at maximum speed and with minimum inconvenience. Under cover of secrecy, they can proceed with their plans even while pretending to observe democratic and participatory procedures. By controlling information, they can make their critics and questioners less effective, obscure the potential of alternative courses of action, and make their own proposals more attractive. The effect of secrecy is very often to make the official policy seem the only real option.

Fourthly, secrecy *covers up the worst abuses of power* – corruption, cruelty, injustice. Finally, secrecy *panders to one of the most uniform characteristics of the powerful – excessive ego*. As Professor Brian Chapman once wrote, 'Secrecy in public life panders to a craving for a sentiment of self-importance – of belonging to an inner circle.' This impression was confirmed by Chapman Pincher:

My long experience of prising information out of Whitehall has convinced me that senior civil servants are afflicted with a pathological preoccupation with secrecy which might be called 'suppressomania' and seems to be incurable. Part of the joy of being at the top is being in the charmed circle of the few 'in the know' and civil servants say that this is what they miss most when they retire. Releasing any information reduces the extent to which they are exclusively in the know.

Chapman Pincher, *Inside Story* (1978)

The decision to deny information to the majority is itself one of such arrogance and cynicism that it can only be the act of someone who feels himself or herself to be superior. Secrecy is a reflection of the 'I know best' type of manager – the 'tell them what to do' rather than 'share the options and decision with them' kind of 'leadership'.

All of this can be summed up as follows:

1. To retain power, the powerful have to appear as flawless as possible – this is actually impossible without heavy secrecy.
2. To achieve acceptance or support for a policy in a democracy, the powerful have to appear to have an overwhelming case – secrecy helps achieve this by covering up the weaknesses in the case and obscuring the advantages of alternatives.

Thus it is my case that the real cause of secrecy in Britain is the desire and need for secrecy of the powerful, and that this is the reason why the Official Secrets Act, so widely condemned by politicians in opposition, and civil servants when they have retired, is sustained by politicians and civil servants when they are in power. This, too, is the explanation for why freedom of information is such an attractive cause for politicians in opposition, but rates low priority when they are elected.

The secrecy mentality

At this point I can imagine the reader crying 'Stop, wait a minute – we take your point, but does the power theory really explain all the thousands and thousands of smaller and petty instances of secrecy? Does the civil servant who stamps "Secret" on a document about cycle safety (as one did) do so to retain power? After all, what real power does he or she have?'

Part of the answer is that, as discussed earlier, he or she is trapped by the machinery of secrecy. Another factor is that sometimes the *only* power a civil servant has is to stamp a document 'Confidential'. A share in confidential information becomes one of the attractions of bureaucracy. However, the broader answer is that the civil servant is probably not motivated by a personal sense of power but reflects the traditions of the bureaucracy, and acts out of habit; and those traditions and that instinctive habit of secrecy are a reflection of the will of those at the top; that will is in turn institutionalised and entrenched by the machinery of secrecy.

Much secrecy is mindless. Anyone who deals with civil servants will know of the extreme caution they show about the publication of any information; as Sir Patrick Nairne, former Permanent Secretary at the DHSS, said during an appearance with me on a television programme, the guiding principle in deciding when to disclose had always been 'the need to know', not the right to know: 'During my longish career in Whitehall one was concerned about the need to know. If someone didn't have the need to know, one should not be passing information to them.'

'Indoctrination' begins on Day One. Almost the first step on arrival in Whitehall is signature of the declaration that states:

> I am aware that I should not divulge any information gained by me as a result of my appointment to any unauthorised person, either orally or in writing, without the previous official sanction in writing of the department appointing me, to which written invitation should be made, and two copies of the proposed publication to be forwarded. I understand also that I am liable to be prosecuted if I publish without official sanction any information I may acquire in the course of my tenure of an official appointment (unless it has officially been made public) or retain without official sanction, any sketch, plan, model, article, note or official documents which are no longer needed for my official duties, and that these provisions apply not only during the period of my appointment but also after my appointment has ceased. . . .

The moment he or she sits down at a desk, documents begin to appear marked 'Secret', 'Confidential' or 'Restricted'. It should not take more than a week in Whitehall before indoctrination is almost complete, secrecy has become a habit, and the new civil servant has adopted the traditions that have developed over centuries.

How to achieve disclosure

To identify the correct antidote to a disease, it is necessary to reach beyond the symptoms to the fundamental cause. If the fundamantal cause of secrecy is, as I believe, its value to those in power, it must follow that we cannot expect those in power to relinquish information voluntarily. That is why the first line of defence of the opponents of freedom of information – that there is no need for legislation, because we can develop freedom of information on the basis of voluntary disclosure – cannot be treated seriously. It is to expect too much of human nature for the powerful voluntarily to disclose information that could undermine their base. It is an insult to our intelligence to ask us to believe that people will voluntarily produce information that reveals their errors, failures or, even worse, their corruption or unfair behaviour. It asks too much of human nature to believe that those in power will enthusiastically make available all the information that could assist those who oppose their policies.

Just as the Official Secrets Act and all the other machinery of secrecy at present make clear to the civil servant that confidentiality is the norm, so its replacement by freedom of information legislation must make clear that open administration is the norm.

The inadequacy of voluntary disclosure is already proven. In 1975 the then Head of the Civil Service, Sir Douglas Allen, produced what became known as the Croham Directive. Its intention was to propose a more open approach, as an alternative to legislation, and it did create the opportunity for more flexibility and disclosure of information. An audit of the effects of the Directive was carried out by *The Times* and the results published by the Outer Circle Policy Unit in 1980. The chief finding of the report was that the Directive did not mark 'a real change of policy' and that only 8 per cent of the documents subsequently released could be described as 'genuine releases' of the kind that would be achieved by legislation.

The Law Society in July 1979 stated:

> We doubt the effectiveness of a procedure for providing access to official information which does not have statutory force. It is an important function of such a procedure that it should be available to elicit information even in circumstances where it is embarrassing to the authority concerned, and we suspect that the temptation to resist a request for disclosure which was not backed by the force of law might prove irresistible in at least some cases in which disclosure is most needed. . . . We therefore recommend the introduction of legislation providing a statutory right to official information by the public.

There is one final contributor to the level of secrecy we have in Britain today, and that is the lack of public pressure for change. Clearly the drive for more open administration will not come from the powerful; secrecy will need to be eliminated at the insistence of we, the people. Why is there not more public demand for freedom of information? First, as I have said earlier, because one of the best-kept secrets is the level of secrecy itself. Second, because secrecy has been so deeply entrenched in the British way of life for so many years that most people have known no other system. We simply accept secrecy as if there is no alternative approach. Campaigners for freedom of information, therefore, have to demonstrate that there is an alternative. We also have to demonstrate how extensive secrecy has become, and how it adversely affects both the individual and the country as a whole. That latter task we begin with the three 'Secret Files' that follow.

PART 2
SECRET FILES

3 HOW SECRECY PROTECTS THE POLLUTER

MAURICE FRANKEL

Considerable general information about environmental pollution – particularly the results of long-established pollution monitoring programmes – is normally available to the public. But the citizen who wants specific information about a particular hazard may be unable to find answers to the most basic questions: Who is releasing the pollution? What chemicals are involved? What safety tests have been carried out on them? How much is discharged? Are legal limits being observed? And if not, what specific improvements is the control authority demanding?

This chapter looks at the way in which people asking such questions are often frustrated by secrecy. In particular it describes a number of areas where information is unreasonably withheld: information about the hazards of pesticides; the levels of pollution released from factory chimneys or discharged into rivers; the location of factories which may present a serious explosion risk; or the causes of oil spills.

It looks at the instruments of secrecy – whether they are disclosure restrictions in pollution laws, or voluntary secrecy undertakings given by pollution agencies to the industries they regulate – and it examines the arguments used to justify these restrictions. The chapter describes the role of the Royal Commission on Environmental Pollution – a constant advocate of greater disclosure – and at the failure of successive governments to respond adequately to its repeated recommendations. Finally it outlines eleven major benefits such disclosure would bring, not only to the public, but also to pollution authorities and the industries they regulate.

Pesticides

The conflicting interests of owners of enterprises and the workers who carry the risks are obvious, but need to be resolved. Making available the best scientific information to both parties may help. *Certainly secrecy has no proper place in the field of toxicology, for only by open disclosure of toxicity data and risk estimates can proper evaluation take place.* (emphasis added)

Professor A. E. M. McLean, University College London. Member of the Scientific Sub-Committee of the government's Advisory Committee on Pesticides.

(Source: *Proceedings of the Royal Society of London, B, 1979*)

Notifiers will acertain and disclose to Departments all information needed to enable the latter to decide whether (safety) clearance (for a pesticide) can be granted . . . Departments undertake that *the information supplied . . . will be treated as confidential; will not be disclosed to persons other than those whom Departments wish to consult and who have given the undertaking . . . not to disclose to any person outside the Committee any information.* (emphasis added)

Part of the agreement between government departments and the pesticide industry trade associations under the Pesticides Safety Precautions Scheme.

In December 1983 the government – after a four-year delay – published its response to the Royal Commission on Environmental Pollution's proposals for changes in the pesticides control system. The Royal Commission had been particularly critical of the excessive confidentiality surrounding pesticide hazards, and the government's reponse included a modest but still significant mark of progress: 'The Royal Commission recommended that the . . . (Advisory Committee on Pesticides) should publicise its work; the government agree and the Committee will in future publish annual reports'.

In itself, this is hardly remarkable. For most pollution agencies an annual report has long been a normal feature of their work: the Industrial Air Pollution Inspectorate has been depositing its account of policy, progress and setbacks on library shelves for 120 years. Yet the Advisory Committee on Pesticides, which has been taking fundamental public health decisions since 1954, has published no more than perhaps seven reports in all – a total output that would fit quite comfortably into a slim A4 office envelope.

The Advisory Committee on Pesticides (ACP) is the key body behind the Pesticides Safety Precautions Scheme (PSPS), a formal but voluntary agreement between the pesticide industry and a number of government departments under which manufacturers agree to market only pesticides that have been cleared for safety by the ACP.

The ACP releases no specific information on the pesticides it regulates:

it will not, for example, say how extensively a particular pesticide has been tested. Not all pesticides go through the same set of safety tests – the testing depends on the use to which the product is put, the amount used, and even the date when the product was cleared. Pesticides cleared ten or twenty years ago may not have been subjected to the kinds of test that would now be standard.

Equally, the ACP does not discuss the findings of any safety or environmental studies on a product: information about a pesticide's hazards is regarded as the manufacturer's private property and treated in strict confidence.

The case for disclosure
There are several important reasons why much greater disclosure of information about pesticides is needed.

First, people who handle these chemicals at work, use them in their gardens, or who may be accidentally contaminated by nearby spraying may have no independent source of information – and sometimes no information at all – about pesticides' hazards.

Independent scientists do sometimes investigate such problems and publish their findings – but the vast majority of all studies are carried out by pesticide manufacturers – and never disclosed.

Second, scientists or conservationists investigating wildlife deaths may be unable to determine whether a pesticide is responsible, because they normally have no access to test results. The Royal Commission on Environmental Pollution reported in 1979 that it had 'received evidence that those concerned with studying the effects of pesticides on a variety of living organisms may be hindered in their scientific work by this confidentiality being carried to unnecessary lengths'. It referred to a 'a scientist who sought information from a manufacturer in following up a point that was put to him by one of our members about the possible risks posed by a particular chemical. The information was refused with the comment that toxicological data, quoted out of context, could easily be used to mislead the public and create unnecessary concern'.

Third, the ACP does not identify those pesticides which it refuses to clear because of unacceptable risk. That information may be vital to users in other, particularly developing, countries to which such pesticides are often subsequently exported.

Fourth, the amounts of individual pesticides made or sold is kept secret – though this would help identify excessive or unauthorised areas of use. Under the existing voluntary system of pesticide control there are no legal penalties for using pesticides for unapproved, and possibly dangerous, purposes – and no inspections to check that this is not done. Dr Joyce Tait of the Open University reported in 1976 that farmers she interviewed were spraying apples, pears, plums and gooseberries with DDT, though the (unenforceable) PSPS clearance at that time allowed DDT to be used on fruit trees only *before* flowering. Since that time the permitted uses of DDT have been further restricted (it is now no longer cleared for use on fruit trees at all) but there is still no guarantee that these restriction are observed. Details of the amounts of DDT made and sold – particularly by region – would help identify whether such abuses were continuing. Such problems were referred to by the Nature Conservancy Council in 1977:

> . . . the whole history of pesticide/wildlife studies is one of hindrance and gaps in knowledge caused by the refusal of manufacturers and suppliers to give figures for the amounts of pesticides made and/or sold in this country . . . there has . . . been a real resistance from certain quarters with an interest in preserving a state of public ignorance on these matters.

The Royal Commmission specifically addressed this point in 1979, reporting 'we can see no good reason why data on the quantities of active ingredients manufactured and sold should not be made freely available'.

Fifth, disclosure would help detect and prevent biased or inadequate safety testing. In 1977 an independent cancer researcher in the US published the results of a review of twenty-three long-term safety studies carried out by pesticide manufacturers in the US and submitted to the Environmental Protection Agency. He found that only one of the twenty-three had been adequately performed and reported. In some studies animal tissues had been allowed to decompose so badly that they could not be properly examined; company researchers had in some cases looked only for tumours visible to the naked eye – they had not examined tissue samples under a microscope when many additional tumours might have been revealed; 'unusual or rare' tumours were sometimes ignored or dismissed as coincidental; and essential statistical analysis of results was done in only one of the studies and in that case, where the company had reported no effect, the independent investigator, after re-examining the figures, reported that the results were 'probably positive for carcinogenicity'. (Source: M. D. Reuber, *The Science of the Total Environment*, 9 (1977), 135–48.)

The problem is not restricted to the US. The ACP admits that some pesticides have been cleared in the UK on the basis of invalid research – though it refuses to name them.

In 1983 four senior executives of what had been the world's largest commercial toxicology laboratory were put on trial in Chicago charged with conspiring to 'defraud clients and government agencies by writing and distributing false and fraudulent study reports'. The US government says that Industrial Bio-Test Laboratories Inc (IBT) deliberately omitted evidence of hazards from some reports, fabricated other data, and then shredded the results when they learnt they were under investigation. A major proportion of key safety studies done by IBT and used throughout the world has been found to be so badly performed as to useless. IBT provided some 800 vital animal tests on 140 pesticides registered in the US – the EPA says three-quarters of these are invalid.

Sweden and Canada have already banned several pesticides registered on the basis of IBT data, and the EPA has threatened to ban a number of others unless valid replacement studies are produced or promised. From the American data it seems likely that at least eighteen of the pesticides registered in the US with some IBT data are also sold in the UK by the same manufacturers, and the total number of such products may be substantially greater.

The ACP says it has identified invalid IBT data used in the UK and where it played an important part has obtained, or is obtaining, replacement studies, but it has refused to name the pesticides involved.

Commercial secrecy

The validity of arguments for commercial secrecy was clearly a question the Royal Commission on Environmental Pollution considered crucial. It suggested that while some confidentiality was genuinely necessary, it was often taken too far. 'We think that refusal to release information on grounds of confidentiality tends to become a reflex action, without specific reference to the question of whether commercial interests are truly at risk'.

One of the Royal Commission's key recommendations was for a review of the PSPS confidentiality arrangements to ensure that information was not unnecessarily withheld. When the government responded to its report in December 1983 that was just one of many important recommendations it turned down.

Ironically, although the government claims the secrecy arrangements are 'essential' the industry has since made it clear that it would be willing to review them. In January 1984, the British Agrochemicals Association (BAA) annnounced that it was prepared to discuss with the government ways of releasing to the public pesticide safety studies and official evaluations of them. However, the BAA insists, as an essential precondition, that measures be taken to prevent competitors making free commercial use of any information released in this way. Such measures have already been developed in the United States.

Explosive hazards

A series of fires and explosions at sites storing flammable chemicals has raised questions about the adequacy both of safety measures at such sites and of emergency plans to cope with any accident. They have also raised a more basic question: where exactly are these potentially hazardous sites – and could the warehouse, depot or factory near our own home be one of them? The people who know – the Health and Safety Executive (HSE) – won't say. The location of some 1,500 sites handling dangerous chemicals throughout the country is an official secret.

Under notification regulations established in 1982 any premises storing or using particularly hazardous chemicals in more than specified amounts must notify the HSE. An internal document on the word of the HSE's Major Hazards Assessment Unit (MHAU) explains to Factory Inspectors how this information is to be treated:

> Lists of major hazard sites are kept by MHAU and at area offices. Because of the concentrated and sensitive information they contain, the lists are classified as 'Secret' and the rules governing the keeping of, and access to, such classified information must be strictly observed. . . .

> Area directors should have sent the relevant extracts under 'Commercial – in Confidence' cover to the planning authorities in their areas. The extracts should consist only of the names and addresses of the premises. Information about the quantity and type of materials stored should not be supplied. . . .

> Under no circumstnces should a copy of any report prepared by a MHAU inspector be supplied to a local or planning authority. . . .

Ironically, the HSE had originally wanted to publish fuller information – but was persuaded to classify much of it under pressure from industry.

Another internal document, circulated in July 1982, discussed the measures needed to meet an EEC Directive on Major Hazards, due to come into force in the UK during 1984. The EEC Directive requires authorities to provide information to people liable to be affected by an accident at a major hazard site. However, only a small number – probably some 250 – of the 1,500 hazardous sites in the UK would be covered by the terms of the EEC Directive. The HSE planned to go further than the EEC's minimum requirements, and publish information about all 1,500 notifiable sites:

> We recommend that regulations covering the dissemination of appropriate information to the public should extend to *all notifiable sites* rather than just the *top-tier*. . . . By this means the public will be able to find out about the presence of all the notifiable installations locally and individuals can make their own choice about the acceptability of the very small risks involved.

The CBI however was not prepared to accept anything more than the minimum demanded by the European Directive, and the draft regulations due to come into force later in 1984 reflect their views. Only sites covered by the EEC directive will be publicly identified – the location of other hazardous sites will remain secret.

Planning authorities and emergency services are being told where these sites are, and employees – who have rights to information under the Health and Safety at Work Act – may learn if their own place of work is on the list from their employer.

But people who have the misfortune to live next door to a site using chemicals which could devastate their homes in an accident will not learn of the risk. Nor will they be told what safety measures – if any – have been taken, or what to do if the alarm bells begin to ring.

Air pollution

In 1863, Britain established the world's first pollution agency, the Alkali Inspectorate, charged with dealing with acid pollution from the expanding alkali industry. A year later, in 1864, Britain chalked up another record: the world's first environmental secrecy policy.

As the original Alkali Inspector recorded in his first report 120 years ago:

> . . . the opinion of the alkali makers, of at least one district, has been very distinctly expressed regarding the propriety of silence on certain points, whilst some have desired that as little as possible should be said on all points. *Of course every information regarding any work must be considered private unless publication is demanded by the Act or permitted by the owner.* (emphasis added)

As industry developed, pollution problems multiplied – and the Alkali Inspectorate grew. Today it is known as the Industrial Air Pollution Inspectorate, part of the Health and Safety Executive. With it has grown the secrecy policy it initiated and has operated for well over a century. Until 1974 that secrecy was self-imposed: there was no legal requirement to withhold information about factories' pollution levels. That was changed by the Health and Safety at Work Act which gave legal backing to the Inspectorate's secrecy policy:

In many ways it was a surprising development, because:

● the Royal Commission on Environmental Pollution had reported – and the Inspectorate itself publicly accepted – that this secrecy does not normally protect genuine trade secrets.

● the Health and Safety at Work Act, while binding pollution inspectors to secrecy, puts a positive disclosure duty on factory inspectors to inform employees about hazards at work.

● the Control of Pollution Act, which also became law in 1974, contains a batch of disclosure provisions applying to water authorities, local authorities and waste disposal authorities. In this context the Industrial Air Pollution Inspectorate's new secrecy duty seemed strangely out of place.

The Inspectorate's refusal to disclose information about the emissions from individual premises under its control came in for sharp comment in a 1976 report by the Royal Commission on Environmental Pollution. 'The Inspectorate's policy on the release of information, even though it is now backed up by legislation, is misguided' the report noted, adding that the 'Inspectorate's concern that the release of such "raw" data might cause public anxiety is often overstated . . . the public should have the right to know the state of the air they breathe and the amounts of pollution emitted by . . . industry.'

The government's reply to the Inspectorate's critics was a master-stroke of bureaucratic escapology. Instead of requiring the IAP Inspectorate to publish pollution data, it gave local authorities discretionary powers to obtain such data, which would then have to be published on a register. These provisions, inserted into the 1974 Control of Pollution Act, were never likely to lead to much disclosure:

- local authorities were only *allowed* – not required – to obtain and publish information; most would have no positive incentive to do so.

- before it can use its powers a local authority must first establish a special tripartite consultative committee, committed to regular meetings. This would have been an uninviting prospect at the best of times – at a time of severe financial cutbacks, it has become a positive deterrent.

From the public's viewpoint, these provisions have been an almost total failure. A survey by the Institution of Environmental Health Officers suggests that only five authorities in the whole country used these powers during 1982, and that between them they were responsible for providing information about only eight premises. Further enquiries by Friends of the Earth suggest that the true picture may be even worse. Four of the five authorities referred to in the IEHO survey denied ever having used these powers, and it was possible to confirm the issuing of only a single notice by a single local authority in 1982.

In fact most local authorities obtain all the information they need from firms *in confidence*. They can threaten unco-operative companies with enforced disclosure, but provided they get the information privately rarely resort to such measures.

In its tenth report, published in 1984, the Royal Commission on Environmental Pollution concluded that these discretionary powers did not go far enough, and called for disclosure of pollution data to be made mandatory. The Royal Commission also noted that the Industrial Air Pollution Inspectorate had in recent years developed a more open policy: for example, it now publishes regional reports with detailed information about problems at particular factories. However, it described the secrecy clause in the Health and Safety at Work Act, which prevents the IAPI from disclosing emissions data without the firm's consent, as 'obsolete and unnecessary' and called for measures giving 'unrestricted access for the public to information which the pollution control authorities obtain' except where genuine grounds for secrecy can be substantiated.

Water pollution

In theory, finding out about industrial water pollution should be an easier matter than uncovering details of factory air pollution. Whereas the Control of Pollution Act only *allowed* local authorities to release air pollution data it *required* water authorities to publish equivalent details about effluents discharged into rivers. But implementation of these measures has been delayed and in practice information often remains equally difficult to obtain – as environmentalists discovered when enquiring about the release of titanium dioxide waste into the Humber estuary.

Two manufacturers, BTP Tioxide Ltd and Laporte Industries Ltd, make titanium dioxide, a white pigment used in paints and other products, and discharge their waste into the Humber.

In 1981 the Anglian Water Authority concluded that 'neither the BTP nor the Laporte discharge has any damaging effect on the Humber estuary as a whole'. This is disputed by campaigners such as Greenpeace who claim that more extensive research in Finland into a smaller titanium dioxide waste discharge released under more favourable conditions has had serious effects on local fisheries, and that UK Humber fisheries have similarly been badly affected by the discharges.

What evidence does the water authority have for its belief that the wastes have no harmful effects? Most of it comes from the manufacturers themselves who for some years have been monitoring pollution levels around the discharge points and, since 1978, supplying the results to the Anglian Water Authority.

In its evidence to the House of Commons Select Committee on European Legislation in 1981 the authority acknowledged that, 'In a situation where the independence of the audit role of the regulatory authority may need to be proven, it is not ideal for the AWA to have to rely wholly on data collected by the industry'.

It is particularly unsatisfying when the data is secret:

● On three occasions the company has been asked for the results of its monitoring – and it has refused on each occasion. Although the water authority has copies of the data it is prevented by law from passing it on; an official who released the information without the company's consent could, under section 12 of the Rivers (Prevention of Pollution) Act, be gaoled for three months.

● The Water Authority also carries out its own monitoring of the effluent discharge: again, it is prevented by law from releasing the results without the company's permission.

● The authority has refused to release aerial photographs which show the plume of effluent spreading from the discharge point along the Humber. The authority says that because the photographs were taken in 1978, 'the situation that the photographs record is no longer relevant to the discharges as they are today'. There is no evidence of any significant change in the effluent discharge during this period and photographs would reveal the large area directly affected by the discharge.

To those involved with environmental problems such frustrating secrecy is too commonplace to be remarkable. What is remarkable is that it still persists even though the government has long accepted that such secrecy is without justification and despite legislation designed to abolish it.

In 1972 the Royal Commission on Environmental Pollution reported that in general such secrecy 'no longer safeguards genuine trade secrets' and called for 'the needless cloak of secrecy' to be withdrawn.

These proposals were later incorporated into the 1974 Control of Pollution Act which contained provisions – so far not enacted – requiring water authorities to enter details of effluent quality on a publicly available register. In 1976 the government announced that these measures would be in force 'by the end of 1979' and in 1982 when this deadline had long expired the government announced that it was now working towards July 1985 as its target for implementation. Even now there are challenges to the proposal.

In October 1982 the Confederation of British Industry told the Department of the Environment that:

> The CBI has considerable reservations concerning the introduction of the register provisions which are not required to be implemented to satisfy the UK's EC (European Community) obligations. The institution of registers conflicts with the government's commitment to minimise public expenditure which has the full support of the CBI. Not only will the setting up, and maintenance, of registers impose additional costs on water authorities, there may be pressures for additional sampling and analysis of industrial effluents simply for the purpose of the registers . . . we are opposed to activating these provisions at this stage.

While the legislation has been delayed, the government has urged water authorities and industry to disclose more information on a voluntary basis. Some water authorities have acted on this advice and have approached local industry for permission to release details about the type and amount of pollution they discharge, and published the results. But this initiative has fallen short of its objective:

● Three of the ten water authorities – Anglian, South-West and Wessex water authorities – have released no information about industrial effluent quality.

● Other authorities have published extensive information but have been prevented from revealing the full picture because some dischargers refused to allow them to reveal data about their effluents.

While the Control of Pollution Act's disclosure provisions have remained unimplemented other changes have meanwhile actually reduced public access to water authority information.

When they were set up in 1974, the water authorities were made subject to the Public Bodies (Admission to Meetings) Act 1960, which guaranteed that their meetings would be open to the press and public. This fundamental right was taken away when the new Water Act came into force in October 1983.

The change does not *require* water authorities to hold their meetings in private – but it allows them to if they choose. And most authorities have jumped at the chance. As explained in Chapter 1, every one of the nine English water authorities has decided to exclude the public from meetings of their main board.

Taken as a whole, the water authorities have provided a telling response to those who suggest that freedom of information legislation is unnecessary and public bodies can be relied on to provide open government voluntarily.

Oil spills

Not only is information about the type and quantity of pollution often restricted, but the causes of discharges may also be concealed. Many of the government's investigations into major oil spills affecting British waters are never published.

The most recent of these occurred in September 1983 when the Iranian tanker *Sivand* collided with a mooring jetty at Immingham oil terminal on the Humber estuary. A 60-foot gash was ripped in the tanker's hull, allowing the escape of 6,000 tons of crude oil. Oil travelled the entire 50-mile length of the estuary and had appeared in the rivers Trent and Ouse which flow into it. The spill could have been a major environmental disaster. The estuary is listed as a site of special scientific interest because of the diversity of waterfowl living there. In Parliament, 18 November 1983, the Transport Secretary was asked about the findings of the department's inquiry into the accident. He replied: 'It has never been the practice to publish the preliminary report on a marine accident. These are prepared solely for internal consideration by the Department.'

The causes of environmental secrecy

Anyone trying to learn about the hazards of a specific chemical or product, or the environmental impact of a particular factory or operation comes up against a series of formidable obstacles:

● there are specific restrictions on the disclosure of information in virtually all pollution statutes.

● many authorities come to voluntary confidentiality agreements with the industries they regulate.

● officials in general are often reluctant to divulge information about identifiable companies or products – even in the absence of any formal confidentiality agreement. In the case of central government employees, this reticence is reinforced by the Official Secrets Act.

Statutory secrecy clauses
Most of the laws regulating environmental pollution contain restrictions on the disclosure of information. Typically, inspectors are given the right to enter premises and demand certain information which they are then required to keep confidential. Disclosure is only allowed if:

(i) the Act itself specifically requires it (most dont't);
(ii) disclosure is necessary in order to enforce the Act – for example when giving evidence in a prosecution, or
(iii) the owner of the information consents to the disclosure.

Statutes such as the Public Health Act 1936, the Clean Air Act 1956, the Rivers (Prevention of Pollution) Act 1961, the Control of Pollution Act 1974, and the Health and Safety at Work Act 1974, all contain such secrecy clauses.

Why do they exist? The most obvious explanation is to protect trade secrets that inspectors might come across in the course of their work.

In fact, most of the restrictions go much further than just protecting 'trade secrets'. The Public Health Act protects not only trade secrets but information about 'any manufacturing process' – so even if the information has no commercial value at all and is perfectly common knowledge within the industry, a local authority inspector cannot divulge it. The Health and Safety at Work Act protects not only trade secrets but 'any information' obtained by an Inspector using his powers under the Act – an extraordinarily wide restriction; while the Rivers (Prevention of Pollution) Act doesn't even refer to trade secrets – but simply imposes a blanket obligation to secrecy.

Several of the Acts so far described are used to control industrial air pollution. Astonishingly, none of them requires the control authorities to warn members of the public in case of a health hazard.

This omission is all the more remarkable in light of the fact that the Factory Inspectorate *is* required to provide such a warning to employees whose health may be at risk at work. But even if the public is directly at risk from the same hazard – for example when workers are stripping asbestos from a public building – the Factory Inspectorate is not required to warn passers-by. Indeed, if he learns about the hazard by using his powers under the Act, the Factory Inspector may actually be prohibited from providing information to the public.

Secrets and confidentiality

Section 2 of the Official Secrets Act 1911 prevents any central government employee from disclosing *any* official information unless he or she has been specifically authorised to do so.

There is nothing in the Act to prevent a sufficiently senior civil servant (or, of course, the appropriate Minister) from authorising the release of any information. But in the absence of such specific authority to disclose, a government employee must assume that all information is confidential.

Even where there is no legal duty to restrict public access to information many control authorities give the industries they regulate a voluntary undertaking not to disclose any information about them.

A secrecy agreement of this kind forms a key part of the Pesticides Safety Precautions Scheme. Similarly, many of the committees set up between local authorities and industry to discuss local air pollution problems are underpinned by such confidentiality agreements.

Justifying secrecy

What explanations for withholding information about pollution from the public are normally offered? The three commonest ones are as follows:

1. The information may be too technical for the untrained person to understand.

In a 1979 statement, the Confederation of British Industry warned that 'Greater release of data enhances the risk of their misinterpretation and the likelihood of unwarranted alarm or ill-founded "remedial" actions . . . data are often highly detailed and technical requiring interpretation by trained toxicologists. . . . This restricts further the amount and type of information which can usefully be released without problems of misinterpretation.'

Some information about chemical hazards undoubtedly is difficult to interpret without specialist advice. However, environmental, trade union and consumer organisations have considerable access to specialists who can correctly interpret technical data. There are no more grounds for withholding complex information about toxic substances than there are for restricting technical information about economic affairs, unemployment, or the weather. Relatively few people understand the raw technical data on these questions – yet it is only because they are disclosed that any serious public discussion on them is possible.

Refusal to disclose information on the grounds of its 'technical complexity' is sometimes an excuse to conceal information which is actually perfectly simple to understand. For example, in 1979 a chemical company which withheld health and safety information on its products from members of the public and workers who handled them claimed that, 'The information is of a highly specialised nature, only individuals with the relevant qualifications and wide experience of the materials would fully comprehend the importance of the data.'

When the company's product data sheets were actually obtained they were found to contain nothing more technical – or indeed more useful – than the brief statement: 'Does not contain materials generally regarded as toxic but accidental spillage on to skin or eyes should immediately be washed thoroughly.'

In 1984, the Royal Commission on Environmental Pollution reported that it had:

> seen much evidence of a growing professionalism in many voluntary organisations in the environmental field and with it an ability to evaluate and present technical and scientific reports which compare favourably with those of officially sponsored researchers. In our view, to deny access to data on the grounds that 'the public' is not competent to make 'correct' use of them is neither a tenable nor an acceptable position.
> (Tenth Report, 'Tackling Pollution – Experience and Prospects'.)

2. Information will be abused by 'extremists' who will deliberately misinterpret it to provoke alarm.

In 1977 an Environmental Health Officer remarked that the Control of Pollution Act's powers allowing local authorities to release Information about industrial air pollution was 'the most damaging piece of legislation ever to appear on the statute books in relation to atmospheric pollution.'

> Action groups, civic societies and pseudo environmental organisations [he said] persistently petitioned and pressurised local authorities to implement those provisions. . . . Action Groups frequently composed of university research workers, lecturers, people who had failed to gain election through the ballot box and including many cranks, persisted in twisting the truth concerning emissions to atmosphere and their predictions of doom were made to the delight of an ever waiting national press . . . He himself worked for a Tory controlled Council which was forever attacked by a multiplicity of misguided action groups, composed in the main of the types of persons he had already mentioned. He believed that any authority which implemented those discretionary powers would drive away prospective industrial developers.
> (From a summary of remarks at the National Society for Clean Air conference, 1977)

It is noticeable here that 'university research workers' – who might well be in a position to make careful and penetrating use of technical information – feature high on the list of people regarded with suspicion. It is hard to avoid the conclusion that it may be precisely because such people *are* qualified to give an independent interpretation that their involvement is resented.

But what of the *genuine* 'extremist'? The truth is probably that such a person, if he or she exists, is only really likely to flourish in an atmosphere of complete secrecy. No hard facts are needed to warn that the release of (unnamed) chemicals in (unspecified) quantities poses an (unmentionably awful) risk which the authorities are determined to conceal by secrecy. Only the release of the data itself will allow such fears – if they are in fact unjustified – to be dispelled.

3. The data will be used to disrupt industry by people applying to the courts for injunctions.

This argument was raised by the Confederation of British Industry in 1979:

> The threat of legal proceedings will be enhanced by increasing disclosure of data. Applications for injunctions at common law could become more likely, putting industry at greater risk of additional costs and penalities even when it satisfies the requirements of the competent control authorities.
> ('Release of Environmental and Technical Information', CBI Statement No. T 559 79)

The opportunity to turn to the courts for protection against injury is a fundamental right of common law. It is wholly unacceptable for industry to withhold information in order to deprive members of the public of this opportunity.

In 1984, the Royal Commission referring to the suggestion that members of the public might cause unreasonable trouble through the courrts, commented that '. . . it is the duty of the courts to recognise vexatious causes and not to grant injunctions where the complaint is plainly without merit. We have no reason to suppose that the courts will fail in their duty.'

Trade secrets

Requests for environmental information are often frustrated by the apparently implausible claim that disclosure would jeopardise some trade secret. It sometimes appears that there is virtually no limit to the kind of information that can be classified in this way – and indeed, this is exactly the point made by those who advise companies on industrial security:

> Whether you make potato chips or silicon chips, whether you sell soap or computer time, you probably own far more proprietary information than you think. The most seemingly trivial things can qualify. The method you use for figuring your bids or running your conveyor belts, or your knowledge of an important customer's favourite cigar, may seem relatively unimportant to you. You may have spent little or no money or effort obtaining the infor-

mation. Indeed, you may have discovered it by chance. However, it's yours, and it may give you an advantage over your competition.

(*Trade Secrets*, J. Pooley, Osborne, 1982)

A real estate firm might consider its clients list a trade secret; a local dairy might put its delivery route in the same category. . . . Every company should have a strict, written policy regarding trade secrets . . . all memos, reports and other written materials should be closely examined before being publicly disseminated to make certain that confidential information is not inadvertently included.

(*Chemtech*, October 1980, 598–602)

Two fundamental questions should be applied to trade secrecy claims:

(i) Are *genuine* trade secrets involved or is the claim merely a cover designed to prevent embarrassing revelations?
(ii) Even when the information does have some commercial value should it be withheld if disclosure is necessary to help protect health or the environment?

Examples of environmental information that has been withheld on the grounds of trade secrecy include:

1.   *information about commercial waste disposal processes.* For example, the company removing asbestos from Fulham Power Station in London claimed to have developed a new form of industrial vacuum cleaner which allowed them to remove asbestos waste more efficiently and cheaply than competitors. But some local residents suspected that the real reason for their low price and successful bid for the contract was that they had underestimated the amount of asbestos on this site. When the residents asked to inspect the device to satisfy themselves that it would not spread dust around the neighbourhood they were told this would not be possible – the design was a 'trade secret'.

2.   *the composition of toxic chemical products.* Industry often argues that the identity of the chemicals used in paints, adhesives, varnishes and innumerable other products is a trade secret which must not be revealed. The CBI has stated that when disclosing information to people at work – as the Health and Safety at Work Act requires – disclosure should be 'in terms of precautionary notices or labels rather than of product composition'.

Without this information, any serious attempts to control hazards is impossible. Only if they know the names of the chemicals used in such products, can users independently check on their hazards; select the safest out of a range of alternatives suitable for a particular job; make sure that protective equipment is effective against the chemicals actually present; find out whether any relevant air quality standard exists for a product that gives off gases or dust; monitor concentrations in the air (it is impossible to monitor an unidentified pollutant) – or obtain correct medical treatment in case of an accident.

A survey of twenty adhesive manufacturers, carried out by Social Audit in 1978, showed that nine of the companies normally refused to tell enquirers what solvents were used in their products. Yet the remaining eleven companies were quite free with this information, and one manufacturer remarked:

> There may be occasions when there is some confidence in this but in general – and I've been in adhesives for twenty-five years – I know that Dunlop and Evode and Bostik products all contain the same raw materials, but the proportions vary and may be important for the properties of the adhesive. . . . I don't think there is any reason why they shouldn't divulge what the actual solvents are or the components. . . . We always give the solvent content to anyone who rings up and asks for it.
>
> (M. Frankel, 'A Word of Warning', *Social Audit*, 1981)

An American official has commented:

> Our office has little or no sympathy with firms which claim that providing the common or chemical name (of hazardous ingedients) will reveal their 'secret' formulation. . . . As a matter of fact, many, if not most, secret formulations can be broken fairly easily using the sophisticated analytical techniques presently available to those who really want to know.
>
> (*Occupational Health and Safety*, March 1978, p. 24)

A number of UK laboratories contacted by Social Audit in 1980 confirmed that they frequently analysed industrial products for competitors and could break the formula of a paint or adhesive for a fee of £100 to £200. Where minute traces of a new ingredient were involved the costs would rise sharply, but the 'secret' would invariably come out in the end.

3. *the volumes and identities of pollutants discharged.* Manufacturers sometimes claim that by studying this information competitors could discover the identity of secret chemicals used, or their volume of output. In fact, there is probably little if anything of value a competitor could learn by studying pollution figures. *New Scientist* correspondent Jon Tinker noted in 1972:

> The notion of industrial secrets leaking away down the plughole is regarded as ludicrous by most chemists. Plants usually have only one outfall, which drains dozens of separate processes, and a firm anxious to protect itself could so treat or mix its effluent that it became unrecognisable. In any case, a competitor wanting details of a rival's waste is more likely to row stealthily upriver on a dark night, and take a sample for himself, than to rely on the meagre information recorded in a local authority's books.

A competitor trying to judge whether manufacturing rates are changing significantly would probably need daily, if not hourly, readings taken regularly over a period of weeks or months. They would get no help from the figures kept by pollution authorities, who at best may take only three or four 'spot' samples over an entire year.

The argument that secrecy about pollution is necessary to protect trade secrets was largely disposed of by the Royal Commission on Environmental Pollution in 1972 when it concluded that, 'As a rule . . . the legislation which protects secrecy over industrial effluents and wastes no longer safeguards genuine trade secrets.'

4. *information about the hazards of new chemicals or pesticides*. It is sometimes extremely expensive to put a new chemical on the market, in part because of the cost of the safety studies that may be required. Manufacturers therefore argue that all information about the safety testing on a new product should be kept confidential to prevent competitors benefiting from it without sharing the costs. To achieve this they insist on an astonishing degree of secrecy. Neither the full toxicity studies, nor summaries of them may be published. Manufacturers will not even say what *kinds* of toxocity tests have been done and the CBI has even argued that 'mere knowledge that a product has been notified to a control authority can of itself constitute valuable commercial information. It may imply to a competitor not only that the notifier considers the product commercially viable but also that the product is acceptable from a safety, health or environmental point of view.'

These agruments have resulted in a total blackout of information about the hazards of pesticides and new chemicals. The public and the people who handle such products at work can often find out nothing about the real dangers of these widely used chemicals. However strong the commercial arguments, such a degree of secrecy should be unacceptable.

But how serious are the commercial arguments anyway? The first point to appreciate is that serious industrial espionage usually takes place at a level that has very little to do with pollution statistics. Companies trying to win multi-million pound contracts from their competitors do not expect to get far by microfilming environmental health inspectors' reports. They are far more likely to buy or bribe their way into the market, often by recruiting key employees from their competitors at vastly inflated salaries.

The Royal Commission on Environmental Pollution reported in 1984 that, even taking into account the experience of countries such as the United States and Canada, where there is much greater disclosure of environmental data, 'incidents in which companies have obtained valuable information about a competitor from the records of an environmental regulatory agency appear to be very few'. It added that, apart from one notorious example where an American agency had accidentally released a secret chemical formula, 'a team from the CBI knew of only one relevant example'.

Even when information of commercial value is released the disclosure may in practice have no significant impact. The original manufacturers of new chemicals, for example, are in practice very much less vulnerable to competition than they may publicly claim. For one thing, in many countries of the world manufacturers of a new product are protected from competition for a fixed period by taking out a patent. And by the time that the patent expires, the original manufacturer has often built up an overwhelming lead over competitors.

Customers already know the brand name and – encouraged by intensive advertising – frequently stick to that brand. It is precisely this effect which plagues the National Health Service, where doctors continue to prescribe expensive brand-name drugs despite the fact that the identical, but unbranded, drug is available at a fraction of the price.

Moreover, some countries do not demand detailed toxicity studies before allowing a product on the market. They may place greater weight on the fact that a country such as the UK has cleared the product, than on seeing the actual safety studies. Thus a manufacturer who keeps its safety studies secret is not in practice depriving competitors in these areas of any useful information.

In 1983, Shell took the unusual step of announcing that they would publish in full the results of their environmental safety studies on 'FASTAC' – a new insecticide which they hope will become one of their best-selling pesticides world-wide. One of the major selling points is the product's 'high degree of environmental acceptability'. For example, the company says that its research shows that 'even when bees fly through the spray itself, they do not suffer harmful effects'. Yet the same open policy does not apply to the long-term animal studies on this product which are used to assess the possible risk to humans. Unlike the highly favourable environmental studies, which can be used to promote the new product, these studies will remain secret and be submitted only to regulatory agencies, in strict confidence.

Greater disclosure, without harmful effects, is certainly possible – given the will. For example, the Advisory Committee on Pesticides could adapt its registration procedures to prevent competitors making free use of published results. It already takes steps to ensure that no competitor obtains any advantage from the unpublished information another company submits to it. Even though it has decided that a product has been adequately tested and can safely be used it requires competitors wanting to sell an identical product to submit their own data – which means they must either repeat the tests or pay the first manufacturer for use of the original data. This is done purely to protect the original manufacturer – it is not necessary on safety grounds.

This approach could be adapted to prevent competitors from making use of another manufacturer's published work. The original data could then be published without any possibility of commercial risk. Such a system already exists – though at the time of writing is not fully implemented – in the United States under the Federal Insecticide, Fungicide and Rodenticide Act of 1978. The Act permits public disclosure of safety studies while at the same time:

(i)   it gives the originator of the data exclusive rights to its use for a ten- or fifteen-year period, and when this period has expired,

(ii) it allows follow-on manufacturers to use the data in their own pesticide registration applications only on payment of compensation to the originator.

Moreover, it is not only the manufacturers who hold essential information about a pesticide's hazards. The Advisory Committee on Pesticides itself produces an evaluation of the data submitted on individual products. These evaluations would in many circumstances be more directly useful than the full safety studies themselves – and could probably be released without the same commercial implications.

Behind the secrecy
If the stated objections to disclosure are so often exaggerated, what else may be behind this widespread secrecy?

It would be wrong to assume that secrecy is necessarily a sign that some reprehensible behaviour is being concealed. British government has never been particularly open, and to some extent remains closed through inertia and because officials find it hard to believe why anyone should want to enquire into the highly specialised technical subjects they deal with. In some cases industry or officials may believe that greater disclosure to a suspicious public will inevitably invite more criticism, even where pollution is insignificant or a problem already well controlled. Withholding data may seem an easier solution than explaining to numerous questioners what the context and significance of the problem may be.

On the other hand, there may well be a very specific point to secrecy: to protect industry from pressures for expensive new controls, or the pollution agency from allegations that they are not properly enforcing those that already exist.

The decision to disclose information about a problem may depend on how expensive it is to remedy. In 1982, ICI scientists published the results of an extremely thorough investigation into the cause of skin cancer in employees making 4,4-bipyridyl, a chemical used in the manufacture of paraquat. Such company investigations are not always published, and it may not be too unfair to ICI to speculate on whether the decision here had anything to do with the fact that the probable carcinogen was found to be not paraquat itself – a highly profitable herbicide – but a chemical present in a now obsolete manufacturing process.

Secrecy by government may likewise depend on the financial implications. Faced with strict public spending controls it may be easier for an authority to suppress information about a hazard than explain why it cannot afford to remove it. One of the earliest leaks after the 1979 Conservative government took office was a cabinet document suggesting that one of the Department of the Environment's priorities should be to 'reduce oversensitivity to environmental concerns'. Officials will not have taken this as an invitation to more open government.

Secrecy may also serve to conceal the fact that many decisions are, inevitably, based on subjective judgement or political considerations. Often there is no overwhelming scientific evidence to justify one approach and reject another. There are substantial gaps in our knowledge of the hazards of most chemicals; environmental monitoring often provides an incomplete or even unrepresentative snapshot of the true situation; and many safety standards give an uncertain degree of protection. Government scientists and officials may be unwilling to expose the way in which value judgements, estimates, guesswork or political pressure have filled the gaps left in the scientific evidence – particularly if they face challenge from unsympathetic critics.

Finally, secrecy may protect an authority that is, or believes itself to be, powerless to deal with problems effectively. This may be because the costs of effective controls appear to be too great, or because the authority doesn't have the legal powers or the staff to enforce them properly. A study of pollution control in two British cities by Dr Graham Bennett reported that:

> Wherever there were differences of opinion between an agency and a company over the proper degree of abatement . . . the parties invariably resorted to a negotiated agreement – in other words, the agency sought to *accommodate* the interests of a company. In this process the local authority often relaxed both mandatory statutory requirements and its own initial demands if these were resisted by the companies.
>
> (*Environmental Health*, August 1982)

A study of enforcement practices in two water authorities in 1977 and 1978 reported:

> It was generally accepted wisdom that control could not be achieved in the face of widespread non-co-operation from industry. . . . Accordingly, where control so permitted, there was a marked tendency to favour consent

conditions which were acceptable to industry, on the basis that such conditions were more likely to attract compliance.

(*Urban Law and Policy* (2), 1979, 337–357)

If a pollution authority loses the good-will of industry there may be little it can do to enforce its standards against a company that is determined to ignore them. Fines for pollution offences are often so trivial that some authorities prefer to steer clear of the courts:

● the average fine for a firm convicted under the Asbestos Regulations in 1979 was £31.

● the seventeen successful prosecutions brought by the Industrial Air Pollution Inspectorate in 1981, many of them for burning cable in the open air to recover the metal, resulted in average fines of £117. The Chief Inspector called this 'a derisory figure by comparison with the profits to be made from illegal cable burning'.

● Genevra Richardson records that one firm had been prosecuted for water pollution offences three times: 'On the final occasion a fine of £100 had been awarded on three counts and £150 on the fourth. Such sums, the officers felt, were quite insignificant and they did suspect this particular trader of having calculated that it was cheaper to pay than to comply . . . some (officers) even mentioned examples when traders had pointed out this very fact to them.' Inspectors in this authority were said to be extremely annoyed at the widespread publicity given to low fines in serious cases and may well have avoided prosecutions that would only have publicised the weakness of the deterrent. (*Policing Pollution*, OUP, 1983)

In such circumstances, secrecy may help to protect the authority from what is perhaps the most embarrassing of all criticisms – that it is unable to enforce its own standards.

Royal Commission recommendations set aside

The Royal Commission on Environmental Pollution has been a constant advocate of greater disclosure of pollution information. Yet while it has had major impact on the climate of opinion, many of its important recommendations have been ignored or ineffectively implemented. In its tenth report, published in 1984, the Commission itself drew attention to this:

Royal Commissions, like any other advisory bodies, must accept the fact that not all of their recommendations will be implemented. However, it is reasonable for them to expect that their reports will be dealt with as expeditiously as the complexity of the subject matter permits. Unfortunately in our case these expectations have not always been met.

Secrecy was one of the earliest of the issues considered by the Royal Commission. In its second report, published in 1972, it investigated the secrecy clauses in environmental legislation and concluded that they had outlived their usefulness:

> As a rule . . . the legislation which protects secrecy over industrial effluents and wastes no longer safeguards genuine trade secrets. . . . It is in the public interest that information about wastes should be available not only to the statutory bodies which have a right to demand it but to research workers and others who make use of it to improve the environment. . . .

That far-reaching conclusion – and others that followed from it in later reports – to some extent helped shape subsequent government policy. Yet as the following brief summary indicates, much of the traditional secrecy about pollution matters has nevertheless continued.

The most positive changes came in the field of water pollution. In its third report, also published in 1972, the Royal Commission called on government and industry to 'reach voluntary agreement . . . that the nature and quantities of all effluents put into rivers and estuaries should be more widely disclosed'. In the years that followed, many water authorities have indeed reached such agreements – and with dischargers' consent have published previously secret information about river pollution discharges. Yet the commitment to disclosure was never complete. Three of the ten water authorities in England and Wales have never released such data. Information about most industrial pollution of rivers in these areas remains secret.

The main impact of the Royal Commission's recommendations was a disclosure clause incorporated into the Control of Pollution Act which when implemented will require all water authorities to publish discharge data on an open register. In 1974, the fourth report of Royal Commission stated that, 'We are anxious that the new measures (in the Control of Pollution Act) should be brought to bear as quickly as possible.' But ten years later these crucial disclosure provisions are still not in force. After repeated delays the Department of the Environment has proposed to bring them in by mid-1985 – yet even this time-table has been criticised by the CBI, which has called for the disclosure provisions to be held back still further.

The Royal Commission's proposals also affected air pollution legislation. The 1974 Control of Pollution Act reflected some concession to the principle of openness by allowing – but not requiring – local authorities to obtain and publish previously confidential information about industrial air pollution emissions. However, these measures have made no significant difference in practice. The discretionary powers have been almost wholly unused by local authorities: details of the pollution released from individual factories is still normally kept secret.

These partial concessions to a more open philosophy were

accompanied by one change that could be seen only as an unequivocal rejection of the Royal Commission's approach. The Health and Safety at Work Act of 1974 subjected the Industrial Air Pollution Inspectorate to a new, all-embracing secrecy clause which prevented it from disclosing any information obtained from the factories it regulated without the firms' consent. 'We deplore this retrogressive step' the Royal Commission reported in 1976, urging the government to remove this secrecy obligation. The government made no response until 1982 – an eight-year delay – and when it did, had no proposals for ending the secrecy.

In 1979 the Royal Commission reported on pesticide controls. Again, it urged that unnecessary secrecy should be avoided:

> The arrangements concerning confidentiality of data relating to the effects of pesticides should be reviewed; information should not be unnecessarily withheld, especially from those engaged in research in this field.

Here too, there was a lengthy period of silence from the government. When it did finally respond, in 1983, it had no proposals for reviewing the confidentiality arrangements. 'A guarantee of confidentiality is essential to the success of the pesticide control arrangements', it reported.

In 1984, the Royal Commission returned, in its tenth report, to the problems of pollution secrecy. It reported that despite some progress, its earlier recommendations had not 'been tackled systematically enough or with sufficient urgency'. The half-hearted implementation of its repeated recommendations for more openness led it to restate most forcefully its belief that secrecy about environmental matters was unnecessary and harmful. It could 'see no case for withholding from the public information' unless genuine trade secrets were concerned. All environmental legislation and administrative measures should be based on:

> . . . a presumption in favour of unrestricted access for the public to information which the pollution control authorities obtain or receive by virtue of their statutory powers, with provision for secrecy only in those circumstances where a genuine case for it can be substantiated.

Specifically, it called for measures that would remove existing restrictions and replace them with positive duties to disclose information. These included:

● a lifting of the 'obsolete and unnecessary' secrecy imposed by law on the Industrial Air Pollution Inspectorate and other pollution agencies;

● new measures requiring local authorities to publish detailed information about air pollution from industry and environmental monitoring and, in the meantime, 'positive encouragement' for them to use their existing discretionary powers;

● administrative and statutory measures to guarantee disclosure of information about all forms of potential pollution including pesticides, new chemicals and transfrontier shipments of hazardous wastes;

● exemptions only when essential to protect national security or genuine trade secrets. Such exemptions 'should be the subject of a proper procedure . . . and not merely left to the authority's discretion or the firm's veto'. A Minister's certificate would be needed and this should 'be reviewed regularly and . . . withdrawn or varied at the earliest opportunity'.

The benefits of greater disclosure

What actual difference would greater access to information make in practice? There are at least eleven positive benefits – affecting not only the public, but also pollution authorities and industry – that can be expected from more openness about environmental matters.

1. Disclosure will allow people to assess for themselves the risks they may face.

Why should people *want* to assess such risks when there are highly trained public officials with a statutory duty to take care of these problems for them?

First, because not all environmental hazards are covered by adequate legislation. Local authorities may know very well that certain industrial processes are likely to cause pollution but may be unable to act until they can demonstrate to a magistrate that a health hazard or nuisance has already occurred. Until 1983, even air pollution from asbestos factories was subject to this singularly inappropriate control procedure (under the Public Health Acts).

Second, even when the legislation is adequate, authorities may not have the resources to properly implement it. Between 1979 and 1982 the staff of the Factory Inspectorate was cut by 13 per cent. When these cuts were first proposed the Chairman of the Health and Safety Commission warned that 'major cuts in expenditure would substantially reduce our effectiveness'. He noted that investigations of complaints or serious injuries were 'already cut to a minimum' and that any extra savings would be at the expense of work on safety in the nuclear industry, the control of toxic and carcinogenic substances, and the safety of premises liable to cause major hazards in case of fire or explosion.

Third, the setting of environmental standards is not a purely technical or medical question that can be left to experts and officials. As the

Department of the Environment acknowledged in 1977 'The decision when and how to control a pollutant that is potentially damaging to human health will always require an element of subjective and political judgement'. Only if they are properly informed can those potentially at risk play a full part in this political process.

Fourth, the common law gives individuals certain rights which they can properly use only with adequate information. People who suspect that pollution may have damaged their health or property, or caused serious nuisance, are entitled to turn to the courts either for protection – in the form of an injunction – or compensation. They can rarely hope to succeed in such an action unless they have the information to demonstrate that damage has indeed occurred, and can identify its source.

Finally, there may be times when individuals simply do not trust the control authorities to provide the necessary degree of protection. Their suspicion may be wholly unjustified, but it can only be dispelled if they are given enough information to assess the problem, and the adequacy of the response, for themselves.

2. *Disclosure may help control authorities detect and deal with pollution incidents.*
Most control authorities simply cannot hope to keep the premises or activities they deal with under continuous close surveillance: they can learn about many incidents only if the public knows enough to recognise and report signs of trouble. This principle has already been acknowledged in the field of occupational health and safety, where disclosure of information to employees is, at least in theory, far advanced of anything available to the general public. According to the Health and Safety Commission:

> We have often stressed that employers and workpeople who are on the spot all the time are much better placed to ensure healthy and safe conditions of work than inspectors who can only make occasional visits. Needless to say joint participation by workers and management in efforts to overcome occupational hazards depends on their having the appropriate knowledge and expertise. *We have no wish to be the only health and safety experts and do what we can to help others improve their knowledge of hazards and ways of overcoming them.* (emphasis added).
>
> (Annual Report, 1977–8)

There is no reason why this principle should not also apply outside the factory boundary. For example, many air pollution standards are essentially *visual* and can be effectively monitored by people outside the premises. Signs of black or dark smoke from boiler chimneys may indicate that the Clean Air Acts are being breached. The Industrial Air Pollution Inspectorate's standards for nitric acid works require that emissions be 'substantially colourless', while many other processes are required to be 'substantially free from visible smoke', 'free from persistent mist', or 'substantially odourless'.

Where excessive pollution is not in itself likely to be recognised informed observers may still be able to detect the practices likely to lead to it: illegal waste tipping, improperly controlled pesticide spraying, or dusty materials left open to the wind when they should be enclosed. Perhaps most important of all they may be able to recognise the symptoms of pollution damage – fish kills, scorches, respiratory problems – for what they are, instead of blaming other perhaps unrelated causes.

3. *Disclosure would encourage public confidence in the work of control authorities.*
Commenting on the Industrial Air Pollution Inspectorate, the Royal Commission on Environmental Pollution remarked in 1976 that, 'Lack of public confidence in the Inspectorate based on the view that their interests are too closely identified with those of industry has not been helped by the Inspectorate's refusal to release to the public emission data supplied by industry.'

However successful it may be, a pollution authority that cannot or will not disclose information about pollution from the industry it regulates will find it hard to convince the public that it is acting effectively. A refusal to provide information inevitably encourages the suspicion that the company is being allowed to 'get away with something' and that the secrecy exists primarily to obscure this.

4. *Disclosure would help improve the quality of government decision-making.*
Public authorities rarely have a monopoly of expertise and there are many outside of government who would respond to greater disclosure by providing information, viewpoints and analysis that might otherwise be overlooked.

At present, such authorities are inevitably judged by those small parts of their work that the public can actually see: prosecutions, product bans, tightening of standards. Yet many authorities would argue that these are misleading indicators of performance, and that the most successful agency is the one that anticipates problems so effectively that these visible signs of enforcement are never needed. Unfortunately, if an authority's dealings with the industry it regulates are entirely secret the public has little basis for distinguishing between effective 'behind the scenes' regulation – and bureaucratic lethargy. It may well be that the greatest victims of pollution secrecy are the agencies themselves, who are unable to take credit for their own regulatory achievements.

Moreover, an authority which knows that its decisions will be subject to informed public scrutiny is likely to plan its decisions more carefully. The knowledge that any oversights, mistakes or poor analysis will be

apparent to – and remarked upon by – outside commentators pro\
unique discipline for anyone who takes decisions.

5. *Disclosure would make it possible to realistically assess the success of alternative control strategies.*

A perpetual source of controversy in environmental regulation is the suspicion that control authorities may not be enforcing their own standards, or may be laxer than comparable authorities elsewhere. The differences are graphically illustrated by the prosecution statistics for different divisions within the same water authority during 1974–77:

> forty-eight prosecutions were brought. . . . Almost 90 per cent of that total emanated from one division. . . . The majority of the other divisions had brought only one prosecution, two had brought none and the last was just embarking on a prosecution policy.
>
> (G. Richardson, *Policing Pollution*, OUP, 1983)

Was this because the firms in one division were worse polluters; because the sewage treatment process there was more vulnerable; or because the different divisions simply had different enforcement philosophies? And if the latter – which of them actually proved most effective?

Another area of major difference can be found by looking at two of the Inspectorates within the Health and Safety Executive. Both the Factory Inspectorate and the Industrial Air Pollution Inspectorate can serve 'improvement notices' on any firm failing in its statutory duty.

In 1981 the Factory Inspectors, numbering just over 600, issued a total of 3,935 notices – rather more than six each. In remarkable contrast, the sixty or so Pollution Inspectors issued only four notices between them.

Why should a Factory Inspector be ninety times more likely to use an enforcement power than an Industrial Air Pollution Inspector? Do the Pollution Inspectors have an alternative and more effective enforcement strategy than their colleagues – and if so, should it not be adopted by them too? Alternatively, is a Pollution Inspector less likely to detect or be more tolerant of breaches of the law than a Factory Inspector?

The Royal Commission on Environmental Pollution has tried to discover whether public complaints about industrial air pollution were caused because factories failed to meet the required standards or because the standards themselves were not good enough to prevent complaints. In 1976 it reported that it was 'remarkably difficult to answer this apparently straightforward question'. Such essential questions might perhaps be answered if more information about the relations between officials and the industries they regulate was available.

6. *Disclosure will help avoid arbitrariness in the enforcement of the law.*
Officers enforcing pollution standards are typically given considerable
discretion. There are obviously good grounds for this: it may be quite
pointless to prosecute automatically for every technical violation however
accidental or harmless it may be. On the other hand, such discretion
carries a risk of arbitrariness. Genevra Richardson's recent survey of
enforcement by water authorities suggested that, 'the variation in the
incidence of prosecutions could largely be attributed to the differences
in the severity of the problems encountered, the political background to
local trade effluent control, and *the personalities of the officers involved*'
(emphasis added).

The discrepancies clearly caused concern within the authority itself:

> Some of the officers were disturbed by this lack of uniformity. They favoured
> a more explicit policy applicable at least throughout the whole Authority if
> not nation-wide. They were evidently anxious to ensure procedural
> reasonableness and advocated the use of predetermined rules to guide the
> exercise of their discretion. They wanted to provide greater certainty for
> themselves and for the traders.

Such certainty would presumably result from disclosure of the guidelines. However, most authorities avoid publishing such information.

Opening up the enforcement process may equally benefit industry,
allowing it to judge precisely what is expected of it by inspectors and to
object to what they may regard as arbitrary requirements. In the United
States one industry body uses the Freedom of Information Act to
monitor enforcement decisions by the Food and Drug Administration
(FDA) and publishes the results in a regular newsletter. The publishers
claim that:

> With such timely information about FDA activity in their district, manufac-
> turers will no longer need to guess where regulatory emphasis is being placed.
> Current information pertaining to the manner in which investigators are
> interpreting the GMPs (good manufacturing practice standards) and, even
> more importantly, FDA dispositions and reactions to real life situations provide
> a basis for decisions to be made.
>
> (Bureau of Phamaceutical Research Inc.)

The attitude of the FDA to disclosure under the Freedom of
Information Act is worth noting:

> Before the (new disclosure) regulations were proposed, the agency retained
> approximately 90 per cent of its records as confidential . . . (subsequently)
> approximately 90 per cent of FDA records have been available for public
> disclosure . . . this policy change . . . impeded neither communication with
> persons outside the Federal government nor internal agency deliberations,
> but had the salutary effect of encouraging closer public scrutiny of FDA
> actions and 'fostered greater public accountability of the agency'.
>
> (*Federal Register*, 14.1.77, p. 3094)

7. *Disclosure will help to prevent excessive industry bias in decision-making.*
When deciding whether or not to introduce new controls over industrial
pollution, the government often has to rely on information provided by
the industry itself. In 1977, the US National Research Council noted
that the Environmental Protection Agency (EPA):

> is inevitably dependent on the industries it regulates for much of the technical
> and economic information it uses in decision making. . . . The situation
> provides a strong incentive for industry to withhold possibly damaging infor-
> mation or to submit inadvertently, or perhaps deliberately, biased data and
> analyses to be used in decision making . . . there are incidents in which
> information has been withheld from EPA, in which studies that might be
> unfavourable to industry have been poorly conducted and reported by
> industrial organizations, and in which industrial experts have not been candid
> in describing problems associated with regulation.
> (*Decision Making in the Environmental Protection Agency*, National Academy of
> Sciences, 1977)

One of the areas where unpublished industry data form the basis for
regulatory decisions is in the safety clearance of new drugs and
pesticides. The IBT scandal – described on page 25 – where pesticides
were approved on the basis of inadequate or fraudulent test data is a
sharp reminder of the dangers of this system. Information about the
levels of pollution discharged into or detected in the environment and
the costs of new controls may also come exclusively from unpublished
industry data. Such information may form the basis of essential safety
standards. For example, the official documentation of the Threshold
Limit Values – occupational exposure limits which also form the basis
for community air quality goals – contains repeated references to
amendments based on 'private communications' from manufacturers.

In 1968 a number of workers at the Coalite company's Bolsover
factory were exposed to dioxin following an explosion. Under pressure
from the Health and Safety Executive the company carried out medical
tests on some of the exposed men, discovering a reduced functioning of
the immune system and impaired liver function. Coalite refused to
allow the report to be published and provided one of its workforce
unions with an abbreviated summary which, according to a report in
Nature on March 6, 1980 'is totally different from the original. In
addition to its selective reporting, the union version says there were no
statistically significant differences between the dioxin-exposed group
and the controls, a statement which is quite untrue'.

Even the Health and Safety Executive (HSE) had been denied the full
report, and on the basis of what it had seen had said that it was satisfied
that Coalite workers had not been unduly affected by their exposure. It
was not until the full report had been leaked to and reported in *Nature*
that the HSE managed to obtain a copy.

After this study, independent investigators proposed a more extensive survey that would include many of the workers not covered previously. Alastair Hay, in his book 'The Chemical Scythe' reports that:

> Coalite would not agree to any further investigations of its workforce if the physicians concerned insisted on the right to publish their findings. Faced with this response from the company at least one physician withdrew his offer of help.

8. *Disclosure would help raise standards by allowing the environmental records of competing firms or products to be compared.*
Very often the best guide to the level of pollution control that is technically and economically feasible is the example of competitors in the same industry. Publication of full pollution data may for the first time give the public, local pollution agencies and often the companies themselves a realistic picture of the standard of control that is in fact possible.

One US public interest group, the Council on Economic Priorities (CEP) has published regular industry comparisons of this kind, returning to the same companies several years later to monitor changes. For example, in 1976 it followed-up the findings of a 1972 report on the steel industry. Examples of its findings included:

> *Armco Steel Corporation.* Armco's cleanup record is excellent when measured against its own 1972 performance or when compared to current records of the other six major steel manufacturers. It now has the best record for both air and water pollution control, and is also the study's most improved company. In 1976 its eight mills released about three pounds of each air pollutant per ton of steel produced – about half the rate of the next best company and one-sixth of the study's worst polluters . . .

> *Jones & Laughlin Steel Company.* J&L shares with US Steel the poorest air pollution control performance in the Update. Its three mills emitted 19.3 pounds of SO_2 per average ton of steel produced in 1976 – over six times the rate of Armco, the Update leader. . . .

The direct comparison of one company with its competitor may provide a far more realistic guide to achievable standards than much of the information that regulatory agencies normally publish. After one 1970 CEP report on the pollution in the paper industry, *Time* magazine reported that the industry association had 'admitted that the report's net effort would be to help speed installation of pollution control equipment'. The *Wall Street Journal* said of the same study:

> Some of the companies criticized said they have decided to increase their pollution control expenditures since they talked to the Council members doing the study earlier this year. A spokesman for St. Regis Paper Co, cited by the study as one of the worst polluters, said the company now plans capital expenditure of $65 to $70 million over the next three years on pollution

control at its primary mills. *This amount is about the same as the Council suggested and up from earlier estimated expenditures of $36 million* (emphasis added).

Inter-company comparisons may be invaluable when deciding which out of a number of competing firms should receive a new contract or grant. It allows a public authority or customer to choose the firm with the best proven environmental record, which may be essential when awarding contracts for potentially dangeous operations such as waste disposal, asbestos stripping, pesticide spraying or the supply of pollution control equipment. Without pollution data such contracts may be awarded largely on price – greater disclosure would make a specific choice on grounds of environmental performance feasible. It would also encourage manufacturers to strive to better their rivals' environmental performance. Under conditions of secrecy such competition is pointless, and indeed competitors sometimes agree amongst themselves not to release information about their pollution levels precisely to prevent unfavourable comparisons being drawn between them.

Greater disclosures would also help consumers choose the safest out of a range of competing products. The publication of cigarette tar levels was intended to help smokers in precisely this way.

Manufacturers of chemical products used in industry have been prompted to introduce safer products by the knowledge that workers' increased awareness of hazards will be translated into new sales. The Health and Safety Executive encourages chemical users to select products on the basis of their safety, a practice which may eventually force some of the more toxic products off the market altogether.

One of the many areas where greater information would help the public avoid possible hazards is disclosure of the pesticide residues found in foods. Although some supermarkets already monitor food contamination levels this information is not disclosed, and customers have no way of avoiding more contaminated produce. Greater disclosure may well create customer demand for 'cleaner' food, encouraging farmers to cut down on excessive pesticide spraying.

There are, of course, pressures against such innovation. In 1978 the chairman of a company marketing spray-on furniture polish proposed to use inert carbon dioxide as the aerosol propellant instead of the controversial fluorocarbons which were generally used. He proposed to draw attention to this in his marketing campaigns:

I thought it would be an added sales incentive. Housewives would see that they were not only getting the polish – but they were getting it in an environmentally safe aerosol. . . . I believe they would see the safe aerosol can as a sales plus.

However, the aerosol can industry was less than impressed:

When I approached some can manufacturers and told them, in conversation, I'd be labelling my can as environmentally safe, they told me to forget it. *They said there was no way they would print a label which implied all the other cans they produced were unsafe* (emphasis added).

(*Marketing Week*, 14.4.78)

9.   *Disclosure would allow companies to police their competitors to prevent them benefiting unfairly from a relaxation of standards.*
For example, Stablex Ltd, a company that processes toxic wastes complained that Essex County Council had failed properly to enforce standards applying to a competing and cheaper method of disposal operated by a competitor – in this case, landfill at the Pitsea toxic waste site:

On several occasions Stablex Ltd have complained to the Authority that wastes containing (a) 0.9 per cent arsenic and 6 per cent antimony (b) sodium cyanide (c) beryllium compounds (d) pesticides are allowed into landfill sites when the site licence expressly forbids them or allows deposition only at very much lower concentrations or rates of deposition. The stock answer is that processing is too expensive.
(Evidence to the House of Lord Select Committee on Science and Technology, 'Hazardous Waste Disposal', Session 1980–81)

The possibility that arbitrary and selective relaxation of pollution standards may give competitors an unfair advantage often causes manufacturers some anxiety. With access to information about competitors' pollution performance, manufacturers – and the public – would be able to judge whether this was in fact happening.

10.   *Disclosure would remove an important obstacle to scientific research.*
The free exchange of information has traditionally been an integral part of the scientist's approach to research, and scientists have reacted bitterly when secrecy has been imposed on them. According to the nuclear physicist, Edward Teller:

Secrecy and science are not compatible. Secrecy impedes progress. Ignorance is bad enough. Ignorance due to secrecy may be incurable and eventually fatal.

The scientist's obligation to share what he or she discovers is held to be of much greater weight than personal or commercial interests in concealment:

Unlike other professionals such as lawyers or government officials, modern scientists have never staked out a rationale for justifying practices of secrecy. They have held free and open communcation to be the most essential requirement for their work.
(S. Bok, *Secrets*, Pantheon, 1982)

Scientists may be affected by secrecy in two ways. First they may be denied information they need for their own research. Second, their own findings may themselves be suppressed.

The Royal Commission on Environmental Pollution has reported that researchers investigating pesticide hazards have been impeded in their work by unnecessary secrecy. A Social Audit survey of chemical manufacturers in 1979 revealed that some manufacturers withheld health and safety information about their products even from scientific researchers. The investigators would receive the information only if they needed it to protect their own safety (when the law would require disclosure) but not if they were investigating its hazards. Even official standard-setting bodies may be refused information. In 1969 the former head of the body that sets the Threshold Limit Values, occupational exposure limits for chemicals, complained that:

> Chronic animal inhalation toxicity . . . data are in short supply because industries do not develop long-term studies or if they do, more often than not do not see fit to release the data in the open literature.

In 1958 a World Health Organisation expert committee on food additives reported that, 'Progress in work on food additives would be helped if more relevant experimental results were published in scientific journals. In many instances these results remain available only to a restricted group.'

11.   Finally, industry too may benefit from greater disclosure.
It is not only the public that is excluded from government decision-making. Industries – and certainly individual companies – may also suffer from exactly the same difficulties in obtaining information.

For example, in evidence to the House of Lords Select Committee on Science and Technology in 1980, Leigh Industries Ltd, a large waste disposal contractor, complained of being denied information by the Department of the Environment. The DoE had not revealed its reasons for particular decisions on appeals relating to waste disposal site licensing applications: 'The determinations are not published and Leigh Interests Ltd have had difficulty in obtaining such documents from the Department'.

In 1975 a *New Scientist* editorial (3.7.75) noted that the DHSS had refused to publish an expert analysis of asbestos hazards to consumers:

> Paradoxically, the asbestos industry could have the greatest cause for annoyance at the DHSS's reluctance to publish the evidence for its recommendations. The industry does not accept that consumer asbestos products are, in practice, hazardous. Its spokesmen say that do-it-yourself operations do not release enough asbestos to cause disease. *The point is highly contentious . . . (but) the asbestos industry has a clear right to argue its case. Yet one of the big*

three asbestos companies, Turner & Newell, didn't even know of the existence of the DHSS report until contacted earlier this week by New Scientist. . . . Not only the general public, then, but the industry too has a legitimate grouse. . . . (emphasis added).

It is significant that in the US industry is a major user of the Freedom of Information Act. In 1982 while public interest groups and the press were, respectively, responsible for 1 per cent and 6 per cent of FoI requests to the Food and Drug Administration, the vast majority of requests – 71 per cent – came from industry.

A number of other ways in which industry might benefit from greater disclosure have already been mentioned:

● companies would be able to check that their competitors are not benefiting unfairly through arbitrary and selective relaxation of standards.

● industry may learn of changes in regulatory emphasis or proposals for changes in the law.

● firms with good environmental safety records may win new business in areas where avoiding pollution is an important consideration.

Ending secrecy
Five basic changes in legislation are needed to remove existing disclosure restrictions and replace them by positive duties to release information.

1.   Unnecessary secrecy clauses in environmental legislation should be repealed; unnecessary confidentiality agreements between authorities and industry should be revoked.
Only information that might reveal *genuine* trade secrets should be protected. Where there may be a serious risk to health or the environment, even information of commercial value may need to be disclosed. The government may be able to prevent competitors making commercial use of such data – for example, by refusing to allow a company to register a pesticide without compensating competitors for their data.

Claims for trade secrecy should be substantiated – a formal procedure has been put forward by the Royal Commission on Environmental Pollution – before information is exempted from disclosure.

2.   Members of the public should have a legal right of access to information about health or environmental hazards obtained by control authorities from industry by virtue of their statutory powers.
This is the principle recommendation of the Royal Commission's tenth report.

3.   Control authorities should be required to warn those affected of possible risks to their health and of the steps they are taking to minimise or eliminate them.

This would merely extend to the public the obligations that authorities already have towards people at work. Factory Inspectors are obliged (under section 28(8) of the Health and Safety at Work Act) to provide necessary information to employees about potential health hazards and about any enforcement action they may be taking. At present there is no obligation on an inspector to warn members of the public that they may be at risk from, for example, asbestos stripping near their home, toxic pollutants released from a nearby factory chimney, or explosive chemicals stored in an adjacent warehouse.

4. *Industry and other undertakings should be required to disclose to the public information about potentially hazardous activities.*
Again, this merely extends to the public rights that people at work already enjoy (under section 2 of the Health and Safety at Work Act).

Such a duty would fill a gap not covered by the control authority's disclosure duties. Pollution agencies may themselves not have full information about industrial hazards, either because they don't have the staff to monitor properly all sources of risk or because they may not have the powers to demand all the necessary information. This is true, for example, in the control of new pesticides, which is based on a non-statutory agreement with the industry and not backed up by legal powers to insist on information.

Parliament has anticipated that a disclosure duty applying directly to industry will be necessary. Section 3(3) of the Health and Safety at Work Act gives the government the power to make such disclosure regulations, though none have yet been made:

> In such cases as may be prescribed, it shall be the duty of every employer and every self-employed person, in the prescribed circumstances and in the prescribed manner, to give to persons (not being his employees) who may be affected by the way in which he conducts his undertaking the prescribed information about such aspects of the way in which he conducts his undertaking as might affect their health or safety.

5. *The disclosure of other essential information about the control of environmental hazards will require Freedom of Information legislation.*
A Freedom of Information Act would make it possible to obtain: assessments of the costs and benefits of various policy options considered by a control authority; the results of research commissioned by a government department; studies of the environmental impact of new developments; guidelines on the way in which the law is being interpreted and enforced; information about the level of complaints received about particular factories or products; and reports of official inspections of premises or evaluations of particular problems.

It is sometimes suggested that Freedom of Information legislation would jeopardise trade secrets or discourage industry from providing pollution authorities with essential information that they have no legal powers to demand. In fact, Freedom of Information legislation throughout the world contains measures to avoid such negative effects. An important exemption to the US Act applies to 'trade secrets and commercial or financial information obtained from a person and privileged or confidential'. 'Confidential' information has been judicially defined as information which, if disclosed, would 'impair the government's ability to obtain the necessary information in the future; or . . . cause substantial harm to the competitive position of the person from whom the information was obtained'.

Some idea of the wide scope of disclosures that would be possible under a Freedom of Information Act – *without* prejudicing trade secrets – can be seen from the disclosure regulations of the US Food and Drug Administration:

> working papers prepared . . . for the World Health Organisation . . . are properly available for public disclosure. . . . Administrative enforcement records . . . will be made available to the public . . . on the basis of experience in the (past) two years . . . there has been no adverse impact upon the co-operation of the regulated industry. . . . It is common practice . . . to write a high official in a company to bring to his personal attention any violation of the law. . . . Such letters have been released publicly for the past two years without disruption of the activities of the agency. . . . A number of requests have been made for 'action levels' used by the agency in determining when it will institute administrative or court enforcement action . . . it is the Commissioner's intent in future to publish all action levels. . . . The Food and Drug Administration institutes many formal legal actions in the courts each year. . . . All legal documents filed in the courts are public property . . . any letters to or from a member of Congress, as well as summaries of oral discussions . . . will be available for public disclosure. . . . Testing and research conducted by or with funds provided by the Food and Drug Administration (will be disclosed) . . . access to all raw data, slides, worksheets, and other similar working materials will be granted. . . . All information obtained . . . through a contract (with an outside organisation) is available for public disclosure. . . . Large numbers of requests are received from plaintiffs' attorneys in product liability lawsuits requesting records relating to any other injuries caused by the product . . . all such adverse reaction reports received on the product involved will be furnished . . . investigations conducted by the FDA of specific consumer complaints . . . will be released . . . after deletion of the (complainant's) identity.
>
> (Source: Food and Drug Administration. Public Information. Rules and Regulations. *Federal Register*, **39** (248) 24.12.74)

4 SECRECY IN THE TOWN HALL

RON BAILEY

Members of the public should be able without extensive research to discover and understand what the authority is doing. This does not mean that the authority should have no confidential business . . . but the aim should be to keep the total quantity of confidential business as small as possible; and to ensure that initially confidential business which is eventually to become public should do so at the earliest, not the latest, practicable stage. An atmosphere of unnecessary secrecy not only makes misconduct easier to hide; it also encourages public suspicion and mistrust . . . the first requirement of any public activity is publicity; the provision of full information on policies, priorities, and procedures, on the rights and duties of all those concerned and of the way in which further information can be obtained.

The more proceedings of the authority are open to public scrutiny, the more obvious will be their probity, and the more difficult for any irregularity to remain hidden. Only if the workings of the authority are reasonably visible and intelligible to the public can there be real public confidence in it. This requires much more than observing the letter of the law on the admission of the public and press to meetings: rather, the authority must present a flow of information to the public, encourage a response to it, and take account of the responses.
(Report of the Prime Minister's Committee on Local Government Rules of Conduct: Chairman Lord Redcliffe-Maude, 1974)

Three city councillors in Portsmouth recently discovered that they could be refused the information necessary to represent their constituents. The city council had prepared a report on conditions in council dwellings which revealed serious defects and a need for substantial repairs. The councillors felt it their duty to read the report in order that they could advise their constituents and take action on their behalf. Indeed, one of the councillors was also on the housing committee and thus needed to see the report to be able to carry out his duties. Perhaps because all three were members of the minority group on the council and would clearly be critical of the council for permitting such conditions in its own houses, they were told they could not see the report.

Members of the public, and their voluntary organisations, are also denied access to information they need in their own interests. In 1978 the GLC set up a working party on condensation and mould growth on the Council's Westbury Estate in South London. However, subsequent efforts by both the tenants' association and the local GLC councillor to discover the working party's findings met with denials that the investigation had ever got off the ground. In 1982 the GLC housing estates were transferred to the local Lambeth Borough Council and the transfer order contained a requirement that all relevant information be handed over. Lambeth Council's officers who were also concerned about condensation were also told that the working party had never produced a report. In fact, it had done and this report was eventually handed over to the Lambeth District Housing Office. The reason for the secrecy was that the report had contradicted GLC policy that condensation and dampness were due to misuse of the property by tenants, rather than to structural defects.

In 1982 the London Borough of Bromley produced a draft town centre plan. A major part of it consisted of a highly controversial new relief road that would cut across an existing residential area. The Council's case was that it would relieve their traffic congestion; the local residents believed less dramatic measures, such as traffic management schemes, would suffice. Luckily there was a statutory consultation period for the residents to put their views and argue their case. Their ability to do so depended, of course, upon their access to reports and information about traffic flow, traffic density, peak hour use of existing roads, etc. All that information and all those reports were locked in the Council's filing cabinets and repeated requests, both verbal and in writing, to Council members and officers met with a consistent refusal to let them see the information.

In Cambridge local people met a wall of secrecy regarding the council's proposed development, in conjunction with Grosvenor Estates, of an area known as 'The Kite'. The scheme involved major demolition of a whole area and attracted widespread opposition and interest. Such was the interest that the residents attended the meetings of the council committee responsible for the scheme. Or rather they tried to attend! In fact for almost 18 months the residents would arrive for the meeting and find that the first item on the agenda was a resolution to exclude the press and public. Finally an agreement was signed with Grosvenor Estates but kept secret. Indeed even the leader of the opposition group in the council had difficulty in seeing a copy, and was only allowed to do so with his legal adviser after he had agreed not to discuss the terms of the agreement with his constituents or any other residents of Cambridge! Eventually it transpired that Grosvenor Estates were to acquire land and property, but there was a 'buy back' clause under which the Council could be required to purchase properties from Grosvenor in certain circumstances. This clearly involved a financial commitment by the council and thus the local ratepayers. The rate-payers, however, were not told the extent of their financial commitment, so they tried to inspect the accounts at the time of the statutory annual audit of accounts. But once again they were thwarted – the accounts were technically the accounts of Grosvenor Estates rather than the council and thus the ratepayers could not see them.

Breaking the law
When the Community Rights Project (CRP) in January 1984 surveyed the way that 61 town halls met their statutory duty to make some kinds of information available to the public, all 61 councils, the majority of them Labour controlled, were found to have broken or evaded the law. The summary of the results can be seen in Table 1 (and the full details are appended to this chapter). Some councils, including Barking, Hammersmith, Salford, Stockport and Sefton failed as many as eight times. Even the best councils failed on two matters.

Table 1. Councils which failed to meet statutory requirements to provide information when requested to do so

Local Authorities – Outer London

Barking...	8 times out of 12
Barnet ...	3 times out of 12
Bexley ...	5 times out of 12
Brent ...	4 times out of 12
Bromley	6 times out of 12
Croydon	6 times out of 12
Ealing ...	7 times out of 12
Enfield ...	4 times out of 12
Haringey	3 times out of 12
Harrow...	5 times out of 12
Havering	5 times out of 12
Hillingdon	6 times out of 12
Hounslow	5 times out of 12
Kingston	7 times out of 12
Merton ...	7 times out of 12
Newham	3 times out of 12
Redbridge	6 times out of 12
Richmond	4 times out of 12
Sutton ...	4 times out of 12
Waltham Forest	5 times out of 12

Local Authorities – Inner London

Camden...	2 times out of 11
City	7 times out of 11
Greenwich	7 times out of 11
Hackney	6 times out of 11
Hammersmith	8 times out of 11
Islington	5 times out of 11
Kensington & Chelsea	7 times out of 11
Lambeth	6 times out of 11
Lewisham	5 times out of 11
Southwark	4 times out of 11
Tower Hamlets...	4 times out of 11
Wandsworth	7 times out of 11
Westminster	4 times out of 11

Greater Manchester

Bolton	7 times out of 10
Bury	2 times out of 10
Manchester	5 times out of 10
Oldham...	4 times out of 10
Salford	8 times out of 10
Stockport	8 times out of 10
Tameside	4 times out of 10
Trafford	6 times out of 10
Wigan	4 times out of 10

West Yorkshire

Bradford	4 times out of 10
Calderdale	6 times out of 10
Kirklees	5 times out of 10
Leeds	5 times out of 10

West Midlands

Birmingham	4 times out of 10
Coventry	4 times out of 10
Solihull...	6 times out of 10
Wolverhampton	6 times out of 10

Merseyside

Knowsley	7 times out of 10
Liverpool	5 times out of 10
Sefton	8 times out of 10
St Helens	4 times out of 10

Tyne & Wear

Gateshead	6 times out of 10
Newcastle	2 times out of 10
North Tyneside	4 times out of 10
South Tyneside	4 times out of 10
Sunderland	2 times out of 10

Avon

Bath	3 times out of 10
Bristol	2 times out of 10

It has been said therefore that most of the information requested was minor. Does it really matter? The short answer is to be found in another question: does compliance with any law matter? If citizens break the law, the authorities are quick to call them to account. Not even ignorance of the law is accepted as an excuse. If the authorities are to impose laws which they expect others to abide by they have to be scrupulous in meeting their own statutory obligations. It matters too because it reflects an attitude. Authorities who do not bother to make available the information that the law has decreed should be available, clearly do not really believe that people need or have the right to know.

The main reason it matters, however, lies in the nature of the information requested. For instance, many councils failed to answer questions about their arrangements to consult with tenants over housing management issues. The purpose of this requirement under the Housing Act 1980 was to enable tenants to have a greater say in how their homes were managed. Furthermore, many councils failed to publicise details of their legal duties to keep houses in good repair, and this can adversely affect hundreds of thousands of council tenants living in damp, leaking, substandard council accommodation. Information on facilities for the disabled and elderly were sadly lacking in some areas, to the disadvantage of some of the most vulnerable in the community, or their friends and relatives who may wish to know what assistance is available to them. To take another example, all parents have a legal duty to ensure that their children are properly educated, and the 1980 Education Act gives parents greater rights to choose schools for their children and to appeal the local authorities' allocation decision. Authorities have a duty to publicise rights for parents, yet many have failed to do so.

Access to adequate information about the activities of the local authority is crucial to members of the public for many reasons. They can make better informed choices and decisions. They can obtain the best available assistance and obtain access to available facilities. They can check on progress in environmental protection. They can ensure that their elected councils are performing to standard. And they can properly participate in local affairs. In short, a well-informed public is vital to a healthy, participatory democracy. Given that people tend to respond to matters that most directly affect them as individuals, you would expect greater interest in local rather than national affairs, and high polls at local elections. In fact, the turn-out at local elections is derisory, and I believe this partly reflects the distance between public and their local authorities caused by excessive confidentiality and a grudging resistance to making available adequate information.

While this spot-check is the most detailed of its kind to have been conducted, it still covered a fairly limited area and further research is underway.

Inconsistencies

From our research so far, there is clearly a wide divergence in the attitudes of local authorities to public access to sub-committees. Some councils do permit the public to attend all sub-committee meetings (while, of course, retaining the option to have closed sessions where really necessary) whilst other local authorities hold all of their sub-committee meetings behind closed doors. The argument of those who have secret sub-committee meetings – that councillors will be inhibited, officers reticent to advise, etc – collapses in the face of the evidence that those local authorities whose sub-committees are open to the public have suffered no penalty whatsoever. This must be the first requirement of any legislation on access to information in town halls – that it permits public access to all sub-committee meetings, albeit with retention of the right to deal in confidence with matters affecting individuals or which for very sound reasons should be dealt with in confidence.

Table 2. Public access to sub-committees (January 1984)

Avon	Yes
Basildon	Yes
Hammersmith	Yes
Kirklees	Yes
Newark	Yes
St Albans	Yes
Wirrall	Yes
Nottinghamshire	Yes in only 13 out of 22 cases
Norfolk	Yes in only 7 out of 22 cases
Forest of Dean	No
Stockport	No
Gateshead	No
Wansbeck	No
Monmouth	No

Table 3.
Local authorities allowing
individuals to see files about themselves

Alnwyck
Braintree
Chester-le-Street
Chiltern
Cornwall
Isle of Anglesey
Shepway
West Derbyshire
West Oxfordshire
Wrekin

The second inconsistency in local authority practice concerns the right of individuals to have access to files kept on them by the council. A small, but increasing number of councils allow people to see at least some of their own files. Maurice Frankel will deal with this issue more extensively in the next chapter, but it should be noted that in this respect, too, the local authorities that have been more open have found there have been no adverse effects. (There is, incidentally, some movement towards acceptance of the principle: the Department of Health and Social Security draft circular of social service files moves in a positive direction, and during the third reading of the Housing and Building Control Bill, in response to a move by Allan Roberts MP, the Under Secretary of State for the Environment, Sir George Young, stated (21 December 1983) that he was 'as a matter of principle, in favour of applicants having access to information' on their files. Minister circular and guidance will not do however; once more the rights of the individual should be enshrined in legislation.

The current law on council confidentiality, as defined by Section 1(2) of the Public Bodies (Admissions to Meetings) Act 1960, is that all council meetings and committee meetings (but, as already noted, not sub-committees) must be open to the public, unless a resolution is passed to exclude them on the grounds that 'publicity would be prejudicial to the public interest by reason of the confidential nature of the business to be transacted or for other special reasons stated in the resolution. In practice what often happens is that agenda (especially committee agenda) are divided into Part I and Part II. The public are allowed to attend Part I, but Part II of the agenda is that part of the meeting held after the passing of the resolution to exclude the public mentioned above. Councils thus have a wide discretion as to what to discuss and decide in private.

It cannot be disputed that some matters are genuinely confidential and that it is true that 'publicity would be prejudicial to the public interest'. No-one can object if a local authority discusses individual cases of rent arrears in private sessions or certain financial contracts where publicity at a given time might result in financial loss to the public purse. It is equally clear however that many local authorities discuss matters in Part II simply because they might be politically or administratively embarrassing, or for reasons quite difficult to comprehend. It is also often the case that matters are referred to sub-committees which the public have no right to attend for no other reason but to avoid the open government laws.

In the metropolitan district of Rochdale all applications for planning permission (except those made by council officers or members) are discussed in Part II after the exclusion of the public. This is surely quite indefensible. Whom does this policy protect? Not the privacy of developers, for all planning applications must by law be available for public inspection (Town and Country Planning Act 1971, Section 34). Thus in Rochdale you can inspect a planning application but you cannot listen to what your elected representative says about it or see how he or she votes.

Many major planning matters are discussed either in Part II of committee meetings or in sub-committees from which the public are excluded. I referred earlier to the Bromley Borough Council plan involving the demolition of houses and the building of a vast new town centre complex. Almost all discussions about these proposals and certainly all major decisions have been taken by the council either in Part II of the agenda of the council's Policy and Resources Committee or in closed sub-committee (or sub-sub-committee!) meetings of the Land and Redevelopment Sub-Committee, the Relief Road Sub-Committee and the Town Centre Working Party. These bodies do eventually report back to full committee or full council so that *after the event* the public can see what was decided. What the public cannot hear, of course, is why certain decisions were taken, or on the basis of what evidence, or what their councillors said. The developers themselves (Wimpey Property Holdings Ltd) have attended some of these meetings, but not the people of Bromley. Indeed the local residents actually obtained more information about what might happen to their area from a two-hour meeting with Wimpeys at the home of the author of this article than from two years of requests to their elected council.

What a far cry this is from the recommendations of the Skeffington Committee which in 1969 considered the whole subject of public participation in the drawing up of local plans:

> Whatever may be the normal internal procedures of the council for delegation to committees and the submission of committee business to the council, the formative stages in the making of a plan should be arranged so that the council can be fully informed of the proposals and of the relevant arguments and considerations. These can then be debated fully and in public by the council. This arrangement may not fit conveniently into existing practices, but it seems to us that the endeavour to engage the public in participation must start by councils themselves dealing with the plan in this manner.

Indeed Bromley's approach is even out of step with the thinking of at least some members of the present Government. In the House of Commons on 3 July 1980 Tom King, then Minister for Local Government said:

> Our policy is to ensure greater accountability and more open government at all levels. The general public will no longer accept tablets handed down from on high whether from the government or councils. There must be fuller discussions on controversial issues.

Reports reaching the Town and Country Planning Association and the Community Rights Project from Swindon, Portsmouth, Merton and a number of other areas suggest that excessive confidentiality regarding planning matters is widespread. Despite the fact that redevelopment plans probably affect local areas more radically and for a longer period than any other decisions taken by local authorities, the public are constantly coming up against closed doors, Part II agendas, sub-committees, sub-sub-committees, working parties and other devices whose main functions are to ensure that major decisions are taken in private 'in the public interest'.

One matter that is often discussed in private by elected representatives is the council's record on empty property. Literally hundreds of local organisations have contacted Shelter and the Housing Emergency Office over the past few years with the same story: difficulty in finding out just how many empty properties their councils own, how long they have been empty and the estimated rate and rent loss resulting. There can be no justification for such matters being kept confidential.

Contrast these practices with a very welcome initiative taken by the London Borough of Hillingdon in July 1978. It decided to open all committees and sub-committees to the public unless there were very specific reasons to the contrary: these reasons were stated as being:

(a) Any negotiations in land, property, goods, services or trade union matters where the Council's negotiating position might be prejudiced by disclosure of the terms which it is prepared to accept.
(b) Consideration or conduct of legal proceedings where disclosure is likely to prejudice the Council's legal position.
(c) Estimates of expenditure for a specific item where disclosure could benefit a contractor or supplier.
(d) The personal or private affairs of any person where disclosure would infringe the right to privacy.
(e) The salary, conditions of service or discipline of an employee of the Council where disclosure would infringe the right of privacy.

Council officers are required to inform the relevant meeting which of the above reasons applies when a matter is to be discussed in private session and the councillors can then make an informed judgement and possibly reverse an officer's decisions. If a matter is to be discussed in secret the public are told of the specific reason for their exclusion.

The public's right to know

Admission to meetings is only a first step to proper public access to local government information. Local authorities spend vast sums of money on research. There are filing cabinets full of information on housing conditions, traffic-flow figures, provisions for the elderly and disabled, educational requirements and all other matters affecting the lives of people in their communities. Yet the public, who pay for it all and in whose name it is supposedly all collected have no right to see any of this information. Many of these reports and research briefs are discussed during the public part of council committee meetings. I have often sat in a public gallery and seen councillors referring extensively to such reports when making speeches. Sometimes sections of the report will actually be read out. The public present, however, have no right to see copies of the reports. In such circumstances to actually make sense of what is being discussed is extremely difficult. Indeed a backbench MP once put this very succinctly, stating that: 'It is clear that when the public as of right attend meetings of authorities they may well not understand what is going on unless they are supplied with documents which make clear the subject matter under discussion.' So said Mrs Margaret Thatcher in the House of Commons on 13 May 1960.

The quality of decision-making would be improved by such access. Take the issue of clearance areas under the Housing Act of 1957: these are areas of unfit housing where the council has decided that the best way of dealing with unsatisfactory conditions is to acquire (compulsorily if need be) all the houses and demolish them. Such decisions are often taken by councillors for the *very best of reasons*: the ending of unsatisfactory housing conditions. Few people would argue with that. The factual basis of such decisions, however, is the advice of the council's professional staff that the cost of rehabilitating the houses is prohibitive. Compulsory purchase orders are issued and a public inquiry follows. At the inquiry the residents present their own evidence that the cost of rehabilitating the houses is not prohibitive. The council officers' evidence has then to be critically assessed in the light of this. Sometimes the objectors succeed and the inspector rules that the public are correct and that the houses can be repaired at a reasonable cost. On more than one such occasion councillors have approached me and said, again quite genuinely, that they are satisfied with the result because all they wanted to achieve was better housing for the public.

But what a total and absolute waste of time and public money. The cause? Not malevolence on anyone's part; indeed everyone acted with the highest motives and to the best of their ability. The cause was secrecy. Had the public had access to the officers' reports on conditions in the area and the cost of rehabilitation *before the clearance area decision was taken*, they could have pointed out to their councillors that there were other facts, costings and professional assessments worth considering. The result would have been the avoidance of two years' delay (that is how long the procedure usually takes) and much worry and heartache by the residents, and a saving of tens of thousands of pounds of public money spent on the whole public inquiry procedure.

In every field of council activity, officers produce information and reports and councillors make decisions on the basis of facts. It is a very common practice that even where local authorities do release information they do so only *after* a decision has been reached. The opportunities open to the public to influence decisions are thus very limited. They can lobby their councillor but without access to available data their case will be weakened. They cannot counter any points raised in the officer's reports. Hence, the need to create a public right of access to interim reports and internal research memoranda, subject to reasonable exemptions.

Access by councillors

The rights of councillors to see information is another whole area where there is considerable cause for concern. I have already referred to the denial of information to Portsmouth councillors, and to the Cambridge 'Kite' redevelopment plan during the latter controversy even the leader of the opposition group of the council had difficulty in seeing a copy of an agreement that the council had signed with Grosvenor Estates, and was only allowed to do so eventually, with his legal adviser, after agreeing not to discuss it with anyone outside.

As a result of the current campaign for freedom of information the Community Rights Project has been flooded with calls by local councillors complaining that they are denied access to information and meetings affecting the interests of their constituents. In Colwyn Bay a councillor complained that information regarding a proposal to construct a waste disposal site in her ward was being kept from her. 'How', she asked, 'can I properly represent the people who elected me when I can't get the information about what is happening?'

In East Devon a councillor told us how he had been refused access to a Housing Sub-Committee meeting dealing with matters affecting his ward. Earlier this year the London Borough of Sutton Council were required to make a submission to the Department of Education and Science regarding the transfer of a nursery school to the site of an infants school. The local ward councillor and Leader of the Opposition Group on the council, plus the opposition spokesperson on education matters were all refused copies of the submission on the ground that 'it is not the practice for correspondence to be made available' to elected councillors. The result, of course, is that is is impossible for these councillors properly to carry out their duties to represent their constituents. Thus the real sufferers of these examples of secrecy are once again the public and democracy itself.

Maladministration

Paragraph 15 of the Local Government Commissioner's annual report for 1983 lists some examples of maladministration in 1982/83 as a result of 'failure to inform complainants properly about entitlement to grants for repairs to a listed building' and 'members given incorrect information when considering a planning application'. Paragraph 27 of the Commissioner's report for 1982 listed as maladministration 'giving misleading information about the possibility of obtaining an improvement grant' and 'wrong information given to tenants that they would be able to return to their homes after redevelopment'. In fact in every single annual report of the Commissioner (or Ombudsman) there have been comments about lack of information, misleading information or withholding of information constituting maladministration and causing injustice. A look at his detailed individual reports provides even more insight into his views on this issue. Consider, for example, a complaint against Tameside Metropolitan District Council. The Commissioner recorded that 'two administrative matters continue to cause me concern' and that one of these was 'the council's failure to provide the residents with documents before the Committee reconvened . . . I cannot see why the residents were denied the documents until after the meeting . . . this withholding of information at a later stage appears as a piece of needless pettiness.'

What conclusions can be drawn from all this? Firstly, that a public right of access to all local government meetings and information (with specific restrictions in certain clearly defined circumstances) is vital to ensure proper accountability of local authorities. Secondly, information is necessary to enable the public to participate in the democratic process and is thus a pre-requisite to proper local democracy. Thirdly, that the quality of decisions made by elected councillors will be improved if more information is available to the public. Fourthly, that incorrect, or insufficient information causes maladministration and injustice. And lastly – and above all – that local authorities as well as Whitehall should be covered by any freedom of information legislation.

Appendix

An outline of the main contents of a Local Government (Access to Information) Act.

PART ONE
Admissions to Meetings

1. The Public Bodies (Admissions to Meetings) Act 1960 shall apply to meetings of local authority sub-committees as well as to meetings of local authority committees and meetings of the local authority itself.

This gives the public the right to attend local authority sub-committee meetings. The right of the sub-committee to pass a resolution excluding the public and press is retained.

PART TWO
Access to Information

2. The minutes of the proceedings of a local authority committee and a local authority sub-committee shall be open to the inspection of any local government elector for the area of the authority at all reasonable hours and any such local government elector may make a copy of these minutes.

This gets rid of the existing anomaly in the law whereby the public can attend Committee meetings of a local authority, but cannot go along later and inspect the minutes of those meetings. It also makes sub-committee minutes open to the public as those meetings would be so open pursuant to Section 1.

3. (1) Copies of any reports being discussed at local authority meetings, local authority committee meetings, or local authority sub-committee meetings, and which are considered during any part of such meetings to which the public are admitted shall be made available to the public present.

(2) Any such reports covered by sub-section (1) above shall be open to the inspection of any local government elector for the area of the local authority at all reasonable hours and any such local government electors may make a copy of any such reports.

This gives the public the right of access to reports being discussed during the non-confidential part of the agenda of meetings open to the public.

4. (1) Any member of a local authority or a local authority committee or sub-committee may inspect and make a copy of any interim reports, memoranda, letters or other documents relating to any matter on the agenda of the local authority or the local authority committee or sub-committee, as the case may be.

(2) Any such document covered by sub-section (1) above concern-

This clarifies the right of Councillors to local authority documents, subject to certain confidentiality provisions.

ing any item discussed in any part of the agenda of the local authority or local authority committee or sub-committee from which the public have been excluded, shall be subject to the same confidentiality as that part of the agenda.

(3) Without prejudice to sub-sections (1) and (2) above any member of a local authority may inspect and make a copy of or extract from any local authority reports, memoranda, letters or other documents which the member may require in the course of his duties as a member of the authority.

---

5. Any local government elector for the area of a local authority may inspect and make a copy of any interim report, memoranda, letters or other documents relating to any item that appears on the public part of the agenda of any local authority committee or sub-committee meeting unless the local authority or the relevant committee or sub-committee has ordered that any such interim report, memoranda, letters or other documents shall not be available for public inspection.

This Section and Section 6 give the public a right of access to internal reports, memoranda, etc., regarding matters that are on the public part of the agenda of local authority meetings, committee meetings and sub-committee meetings. However, the authority or relevant committee or sub-committee can pass a resolution in cases of confidentiality being required restricting this right of the public.

---

6. Any such order as referred to in Section 5 above shall only be made on the grounds that public access to the documents referred to in that Section would be an invasion of personal privacy or detrimental to the public interest, but not because such public access would be politically or administratively embarrassing to the local authority or any member or officer of the local authority.

---

7. It shall be the duty of a local authority to publish a list of the names and addresses of all members of the authority and all members of any committee or sub-committee of the authority and any local government elector for the area of the

This requires a local authority to publish the names and addresses of Councillors (they are already published in the Municipal Year Book for those who know the system) and enables electors to have a copy of this list.

local authority may at all reasonable hours inspect and make a copy
of any such list.

8. It shall be the duty of a local authority to publish a summary of the
rights of local government electors
to attend meetings and inspect documents of local authorities given by
this Act or by the Public Bodies
(Admissions to Meetings) Act
1960 or by the Local Government
Act 1972 and any local government elector for the area of the
local authority may at all reasonable hours inspect and make a copy
of any such summary.

**This requires local authorities to
publish a summary of the public's
rights of access to meetings and documents and enables electors to have a
copy of this summary.**

Note: This is the outline Bill prepared by the Community Rights Project which,
in 1984, is being promoted by three MPs: Allan Roberts (Labour), Simon
Hughes (Liberal), and Robin Squire (Conservative).

5 FILES ON OURSELVES – FACT OR FICTION?

MAURICE FRANKEL

Public authorities provide a considerable range of services and benefits to those whom they judge to be in need or entitled to them. Moreover, they exercise great power over our lives in other ways: in levying taxes, granting permits or licences of various kinds, or enforcing compliance with a wide range of laws.

The basis for many decisions is the vast numbers of records kept about us in official filing cabinets or – increasingly now – on computers. The official or clerk who transfers information from the file to the form and back again may perceive his job as relatively unimportant: but the quality of his record-keeping may be crucial to our welfare. Yet it is so easy for the information to be wrong. Even the most scrupulous decision-taker may be working with information recorded over a period of years by a succession of note-takers, working to an unspecified and unknowable degree of precision. A number misheard on the phone, a note compiled from an out-of-date form, or an incorrectly transcribed figure may totally distort the evidence on the file.

This information is at least relatively straightforward to verify. Many decisions, however, are based on information that is inevitably more complex because it draws on the professional evaluation of circumstances, abilities or difficulties of the person concerned. Is a family really in need of new accommodation? Is a medical condition serious enough to require immediate treatment – or sufficiently debilitating to disqualify the person from work? Is a child safe in his or her home – or at such risk of abuse that he ought to be taken into care? Is an elderly or handicapped person capable of looking after him or herself alone? Would that person become so if given additional support or benefits? Is a child's poor progress at school the result of poor ability or an unsympathetic environment? Is someone's strange behaviour the result of psychiatric illness – or is it a response to some unnoticed provocation?

All these decisions may rely heavily on the judgement of teacher, doctor, social worker or other professionals involved. Yet, even their training cannot guarantee that they will not occasionally misunderstand what is being said, misinterpret what they see, or overlook what the person they are dealing with assumes they already know. Although the wrong decision may have a devastating effect on the lives of those involved, it is impossible to eliminate errors, oversights or misjudgements of this kind. It is, though, possible to put many of them right before they seriously harm the individuals concerned, for if individuals have the right to see the files held about them, and can question or correct inaccurate information they find there, many of the serious abuses described in this chapter can be prevented.

The principle of opening records to their subjects (though not to anyone else) is already laid down in the Data Protection Bill going through Parliament at the time of writing. Yet the Bill's scope is very limited: it applies only to computerised records, not to those held on paper, and important areas of records may be exempted from access altogether.

This chapter looks in detail at three major areas: education, health, and social work. It describes not merely the problems but the grave injustices that many have suffered as a result of the information or assessments held on their files, acted on by the school, surgery or department – and sometimes circulated to others outside – but kept secret from the person they most directly affect.

Education

School reports on pupils
In the vast majority of local education authorities, school records are kept secret from parents and the young people they concern. Yet the information on them may be crucial to decisions that affect the pupil's education: which stream he or she will be put into, the courses or examinations the pupil is able to take, or the reference the school may provide to an employer or university.

The contents of a school record may have even wider-reaching effects, influencing other agencies that deal with – and may have considerable power over – not only the young person, but also his or her family. Information from a pupil's record is commonly passed on to education welfare officers, educational psychologists and careers advisers, social workers and probation officers. Some heads pass records on to prospective employers. Some allow police access to pupils' records.

The Advisory Centre for Education (ACE) – which has contributed much of the material used in this section – argues that this secrecy 'protects unreasonable headteachers. It gives them the power to ignore a parent's point of view and the power to act against the best interests of a pupil or student.' Of course, not all heads are unreasonable, yet ACE suggests that the cases below are not untypical.

'Worst report ever seen'
About two years ago, Brian was assaulted by a teacher at his school. His parents complained to the head, who assured them that the teacher would be reprimanded. Then, a few months ago, it happened again. The same teacher caught hold of Brian by the neck, causing a friction burn and bruising. The boy ran home and his father took him to the police station. The police advised the parents to take out a charge of assault on the teacher.

Unfortunately, Brian's father lost his temper and went to the school to see the teacher. Finding him in the dining hall he lifted him up by the lapels and threatened him. The head of the school immediately suspended Brian.

The parents appealed against the suspension. At the governors' meeting the head read from a report a long list of incidents of bad behaviour on Brian's part. The parents were not given a copy. They argued that if their son's behaviour had been so bad for such a long time, they should have been informed. They also showed the governors their son's end of term report, written only two weeks before the suspension. It was nothing like the report which the head read out. According to the report, Brian was not badly behaved; his work was 'improving'. Nevertheless, the head said he wanted Brian expelled. In the end, that is what happened.

Paul McNamee, a founder of the (no longer active) Campaign Against Secret Records on School Children, has described in 'The Paper Chain' (an unpublished manuscript), other examples, including the one below, where incorrect information on pupils' records has had serious consequences:

A highly intelligent girl of ten was unhappy in primary school, so was sent by her father (a head teacher) to a private boarding school until she was thirteen. She was happy there and made good progress at her work. Her father then decided that it was time for her to follow the example of her older sister and finish her secondary education at the local grammar school – the older girl had passed from there to university and to a distinguished academic career. He accordingly applied for a place for his daughter at the grammar school and was considerably astonished when this was refused.

He set about putting matters right and in due course obtained an interview with an education official at County Hall. The official told him his daughter was unsuited to the academic type of education provided by a grammar school. On being pressed the official admitted that the basis for this decision was something that had appeared in the child's record when she was ten.

The father asked to see the record; he was not surprised when this was refused, for the head of the child's boarding school had seen the record and had described it to the father as 'vitriolic'. When he suggested, with the authority of considerable experience to back him up, that a child can change a good deal between ten and thirteen, he was told that this was not true: a child's character had become fixed by nine. When the head then suggested that the record ought to be destroyed the official registered shock. The records were authority property and could not be destroyed. The father told the writer that he would have to complete his younger daughter's education privately, at considerable expense.

Occasionally parents have managed to see the record cards. One mother discovered a card describing her daughter as a 'vandal' and 'delinquent'. She was able to trace the entry to a single incident, a squabble in a cloakroom in her daughter's school. The following entries contradict the image of the teacher painstakingly concerned to record only the exact truth:

'A's unhygienic habits make her an isolate.'

'C is a compulsive thief.'

'D's parents are not married' (they had been for some years).

'A quiet, down-at-heel little girl.'

'A high IQ figure . . . surprising in a child from a dull family.'

'This girl is a thief and a liar and sly' (a girl aged nine; another teacher said of this girl, 'During her sojourn with us (she) proved honest, truthful, frank and extremely helpful at all times').

'A has vicious tendencies' (a girl of nine; her next teacher failed to find them).

'Religion is Mormon, it hasn't helped the situation.'

'Has little to say . . . home provides little stimulus for conversation' (a child of six).

'Very difficult, naughty boy' (aged five).

'Dirty sexual habits' (a boy of ten – one incident which took place on a beach), a similar entry on a boy who exposed himself in a playground – he was five.

'A bit concerned over S's honesty, though as yet no evidence.'

'Very much a tomboy – latest interest is motor-bikes' (the space in which this entry appeared was headed, 'Significant medical information').

'X has a reputation for petty theft, which we are sure of, but there is a lack of proof in several cases.'

'Pasty, podgy, vacant, moribund, harmless, frustrating' (a boy from a poor area).

Taking the above entries as a whole it is easy to sense the thoughtlessness and careless haste with which these comments are recorded. Many of the entries are based on opinion, hearsay or prejudice; they probably reflect the strains of the teacher's day, with its frustration, anger or annoyance, as much as the truth about the children they describe.

With records of this kind it is not surprising that some local education authorities (LEAs) may deny their very existence. In 1978 Marie Macey of Bradford University described her efforts to carry out some basic research into school record keeping. She had written to forty-two LEAs asking for basic factual information – such as copies of the blank forms on which pupil records were kept. 'The majority of those requested categorically refused to supply the information requested . . . the actual existence of (such records) . . . were denied in many cases. In other areas where standardised record keeping was acknowledged to exist officials refused to let me see a blank record card, and I was amazed at how many areas had their record cards either "under review" or "at the printer"' (Advisory Centre for Education, WHERE, May 1978).

All schools and local education authorities (LEAs) in this country keep records on individual school students. These records contain information about educational attainment, some medical details, and often comments about the student's social and family background, behaviour, personality and predictions about future 'potential'. The way in which information is recorded varies from one LEA to another. Files may contain letters from one professional to another, brief observations by an individual teacher, examination results, etc. Some LEAs have introduced standardised record cards containing a list of categories which the teacher merely has to tick. The records start as soon as children enter nursery or infant school and will accompany them throughout their school life, transferring with them from one school to another. They are used to prepare references for jobs and further and higher education, and are particularly relied upon in large schools where the teacher or headteacher writing the reference has had little personal contact with the student. Records are kept at the school, and often also at the LEA offices. They may be passed to (and contain comments from) welfare officers, social workers, psychologists, career advisers – and in some cases even the police.

Parents and school students, however, have no legal right to see their own records. Nor do they have any control over who else has access to the files.

LEAs do not, and should not, need to be forced by law to adopt open record policies. However, in the five years since ACE's first survey of LEA record keeping policies (which revealed that no LEA gave parents guaranteed access to all records and reports) very few LEAs have adopted such a policy.

A few LEAs have issued guidelines to their schools suggesting that parents should have limited access to certain kinds of information (e.g. Manchester) but on the whole it is left to the 'discretion' of individual headteachers to decide who should and who should not see records – which means, in practice, that records pass freely between the various agencies which may be involved in the student's 'welfare', but are withheld from parents.

In October 1983 Brent Education Authority decided to open its school records to parents.
Teachers will transfer information from the present school record cards (all 45,000 of them) on the newly devised forms. Information which staff felt could not be shown to parents will be destroyed. At the end of the summer term 1984, parents will be sent a copy of the school record form for their child. This will take the place of the end of year report. A covering letter will explain that schools also have letters (from doctors, social workers, educational psychologists, etc) on file and that parents have the right to ask to see any letter relating to their own child.

Doctors, social workers and educational psychologists will all be told that in future the letters which they send to schools in relation to particular pupils will not be confidential, but will be shown to the parents and guardians of the pupils. Students over the age of 18 are being given the same right of access as their parents.

The coming into effect of the 1981 Education Act, on 1 April 1983, added extra impetus to the policy discussions in Brent.

Parents of children with 'Statements of Special Education Needs' are given access to all the professional reports, including social work reports, used by the local education authorities in making decisions about their children. Brent was keenly aware that if they did not open up all school records, an unequal and unfair outcome would result, with the parents of children with special needs having more rights in terms of access to official documents than parents of children without special needs (Source: *WHERE*, October 1983).

In February 1984, the Inner London Education Authority decided that records on pupils admitted to secondary schools from September 1984 would become available to parents.
Parents of children in ILEA primary schools have been able to see their school records since 1976. The new decision will gradually extend this policy to secondary schools. However, secondary records compiled before this policy takes effect will not be subject to disclosure.

Elsa Davies, the headteacher of a primary school in Stanmore, has described the way in which formerly secret records at her school have been opened to parents and to pupils themselves:

A contributory factor to this decision was our view of the pupil as a person capable of self determination and deserving of the right to information which enabled him to exercise this capacity. We followed this decision by taking the next logical step which was to provide the opportunity for children and parents to add to these school notes. The position now is that the three parties most closely concerned with a child's education, namely, the pupil, the parents and the teacher, work together to produce a vital, worthwhile, working document . . .

This new procedure began as a result of experience with individual children. When a child with a particular difficulty was mentioned to me by a teacher, an opportunity was made for me to talk privately with the pupil. On these occasions, the school records were to hand and if the pupil agreed, we examined his notes for knowledge relevant to our discussion. The information contained in the notes sometimes acted as a catalyst in drawing discussion towards a constructive outcome. On more than one occasion it was observed that until a pupil had been made aware of the contents of his notes, he did not fully appreciate the seriousness of his difficulty nor indeed, the quality of his strengths and latent talents. Through providing the opportunity for discussing perceived problems constructively, pupils come to realise that the decision to act for improvement is theirs alone. Only by making people aware of this personal responsibility can they grow in the understanding of their ability to control their learning, development and ultimately, their own destinies.

As a result of experience with particular children, it was decided to take a more positive approach in using the pupil notes as learning devices. In 1981, I began to hold private discussions or 'interviews' with pupils in our oldest year group (7–8 years). During these 'interviews' the pupil and I discuss both academic progress and general social and emotional development including any particular area of concern to the pupil. The depth and breadth of many of these sessions confirmed my belief in the high degree of self perception and self criticism latent in the child . . .

From a more academic viewpoint, the 'pupil interview' provides an ideal opportunity for encouraging the child to plan ahead. Not only are pupils able to express how they feel about past achievement but they are also encouraged to predict their progress over a certain period . . .

These private interviews with pupils also provide the opportunity for making children aware of the need to direct their efforts to best effect. Many children spend their schooldays practising that which they do well, when they really need to come to terms with aspects of learning which they may find difficult to grasp. It goes without saying that the attention of children is drawn to their strengths: it is also drawn to areas which need practice or consideration. By identifying the problem together, discussing learning strategies and sometimes agreeing a programme of action, pupils are encouraged to achieve their fullest potential . . .

Our programme is founded on the most basic principle of all that, strange as it may seem to say it, children are people and that, whatever their age, they are deserving of the right to be involved in the planning and organisation of experiences presented to them. It is only through such involvement that people grow in their ability to decide their courses of action, become dependent on their inner resources, develop creativity of spirit and become self-confident and capable persons. By according respect and dignity to the pupil in the way we do, we may hope to achieve the most precious outcome of all, namely, a young person conscious of his own potential and possessor of an honest and healthy self image.

School reports and the juvenile courts

One area where secret records may regularly be causing serious injustice is the juvenile courts. These are special courts where criminal proceedings against young people aged between ten and sixteen are heard. Although for many offenders the penalties imposed by these courts are relatively minor – regular visits to an attendance centre on Saturday afternoons, or a curfew – there can be much more serious consequences: a period of custody at a detention centre, or a care order.

Before sentencing juvenile courts take into account a school report which local authorities have a statutory duty to submit. These school reports may be extremely influential. A small survey of care orders made in a single juvenile court between 1977 and 1978 identified educational or school factors as the 'primary factor' in influencing the court's decision in eleven out of twenty care orders.

The school report may be crucial legal evidence – yet it is often kept secret both from the pupil and his or her parents.

Access to these reports is governed by the Magistrates' Courts (Children and Young Persons) Rules 1970. Rule 10 states that any written report from a doctor, probation officer or local authority – the latter would submit a school report – 'may be received and considered by the court without being read aloud'.

If the court decided not to read out the full report, the child and his or her parents should be told of any relevant information in it. The rules state explicitly:

Where . . . a report has been considered without being read aloud . . . the child or young person shall be told the substance of the information given to the court bearing on his character or conduct which the court considers to be material to the manner in which the case should be dealt with unless it appears to be impracticable to do so having regard to his age and understanding.

Having heard this evidence, the offender is given the opportunity to reply or submit further evidence before sentencing takes place.

Caroline Ball of the University of East Anglia has examined the ways in which these disclosure rules are applied. In 1983, she reported that court practice varies 'from scrupulous adherence to total non-compliance' adding that the provisions are 'fairly regularly either misunderstood or ignored' ('Secret Justice: The Use Made of School Reports in the Juvenile Court.' *British Journal of Social Work* (1983), **13**, 197–206).

A 1981 questionnaire survey of clerks of juvenile courts revealed that 59 per cent of courts did not show school reports to parents or defendants. In the 41 per cent with a more open policy, over half confined disclosure to parents. Where reports are not fully disclosed, the rules require that relevant extracts be read out or summarised. The disturbing evidence of Caroline Ball's survey is that 32 per cent of courts 'seldom' or 'never' did this.

She reported there was a 'total failure to obey the rules in that the chairman did not refer to the contents of the reports, even in vague terms, until he was passing sentence, giving no opportunity for the defendant or the panel to dispute any allegations made'. Such practices clearly permit serious abuses – indeed, the clerk in one of the courts which did not normally show school reports remarked, 'I am unhappy at the sense that some secret justice could be taking place'.

A working party set up by the National Association for the Care and Resettlement of Offenders (NACRO) reported in 1984 that:

> all present had experience of school reports which contained unsubstantiated allegations of criminal behaviour as well as extreme and damaging remarks about conduct and character which amounted to expressions of exasperation stated as fact . . . teachers frequently yield to the understandable temptation to use the school report to the court as a forum for the expression of frustration about, or even irritation/anger towards a child, especially a child who is a nuisance in school . . . a school may see the pending court appearance of a pupil as an opportunity to get rid of a troublemaker.
>
> ('School Reports in the Juvenile Courts', NACRO, 1984)

To a certain extent, the report forms used by education authorities may themselves encourage schools to focus a pupil's difficulties, failures or weaknesses. NACRO found that 'out of a random sample of forty different report forms there was only one which asked positively for the report writer to say something good about the pupil. Report forms in general appear to be framed in the expectation of a negative comment.'

Although the reports are intended for the courts, there is nothing to stop the schools themselves releasing them to the pupils concerned or their parents. However, NACRO found only four local authorities in the country with a positive policy of disclosing these reports. A further 18 per cent did however say that disclosure was standard practice, although not formal policy. Other local authorities said the question was left to the discretion of head teachers, but the majority 'appear to treat the reports as confidential documents prepared for the court and would not allow their contents to be revealed to parents and children prior to the court proceedings'.

Although some courts have moved towards greater disclosure in recent years, others have gone in the opposite direction. The imposition of greater restrictions was attributed by court clerks mainly to pressure from head teachers. 'Comments to the effect that head teachers, when they discovered that courts were showing their reports, "were not at all pleased and following a meeting the practice was changed", were made by several clerks.'

University secrecy

The process of secret evaluation does not end when the pupil leaves school. At university, even mature post-graduate students – who may in some cases be older than their tutors – have no right to see the academic assessments made on their work, though these, if unfavourable, may blight their career.

For institutions that place such weight on intellectual integrity, universities show an astonishing reluctance to explain how assessments are reached – or to allow the student to question one that he or she believes to be inadequate or biased. For example, London University's regulations include the following remarkable restrictions on disclosure:

Publication of Examination Results
The marks obtained by candidates must at all times be regarded as strictly confidential to the examiners and the Responsible Officer. No marks are to be put on material which is likely to be returned to the candidate . . .

The Academic Registrar may on request from a School or Senate Institute authorise the release of marks by the examiners to the Appointed or Recognised Teacher or School or Institute concerned. Any marks so communicated are issued in the strictest confidence and are for use of Teachers and Schools or Institutes only for their own information in assessing the progress of their students and may not be further revealed . . .

In advising a student, Teachers and Schools or Institutes may give only general information relating to the examination performance of the candidate. On no account is specific information on marks to be passed on to a student.
('Instructions for the Appointment of Examiners and Conduct of Examinations for M Th, MA, LLM, M Mus, M Sc, and M Ed Degrees')

Students whose masters or doctoral theses are rejected by the examiners are similarly given no specific information about the reasons for the assessment. According to a letter from Miss J. Vijayatunga, whose PhD thesis was rejected by London University in 1979:

To date I have not been allowed to challenge the examiners; I have been given no explanation as to why my thesis should not be up to PhD standard; the University has not disclosed even a gist of the examiners' reports . . . it is my submission that:
(a) One undertakes a period of professional training at great personal sacrifice and hardship. It follows that one should at the very least be given an explanation.
(b) If one does not know what the examiners have said, how is one expected to improve in future?
(c) The examiners' reports are of interest to the candidate and to no one else . . .
(d) The examiners are paid to give an 'objective' assessment/professional assessment. It follows that not only should they be in a position to counteract any criticism but they should welcome the opportunity of doing so.

The injustice of this secrecy becomes all the more apparent when contrasted with the scrupulous safeguards provided for academic staff themselves. A lecturer, who may be appointed for an initial probationary period of up to three years, is guaranteed immediate access to any unfavourable reports from his or her superior, with full rights to question them or have them independently evaluated:

> If other than wholly satisfactory, the reports of the Head of Department with observations by the Director where appropriate, will cover all aspects of the probationer's work and will be made available to him in writing at the time. Such a report will indicate specific defects and must include remedial advice to help him to make his work satisfactory. It is the duty of the Head of Department and the Director to discuss unsatisfactory reports with a probationer and he is entitled to receive as soon as practicable afterwards an agreed written note of the discussion. He will be entitled to make written comments on these reports and also to ask for a more detailed independent written report from his adviser to be included in his probationary record.
> (Typical University of London Terms of Employment for an academic post subject to a probationary period)

Secrecy inevitably suggests that someone somewhere has something to hide. What the universities may be hiding is that they sometimes fail to provide their students with the essential ingredients of a proper education: adequate tuition and a fair examination. Moreover, the student who – after years of solitary research – believes he has unjustly suffered in this way is often also deprived of a third crucial element: the right to make an informed appeal.

Post-graduate students have a notoriously high failure rate. In 1983, a joint committee of the Science and Engineering Research Council and the Social Science Research Council found that only one in five PhD students had completed their thesis at the end of four years, though their grants would normally have expired after three.

A Department of Education survey revealed that 42 per cent of PhD students in the humanities had failed to gain their degree *ten years later*. These 'wholly unsatisfactory' completion rates were not the fault of the candidates themselves, according to the Advisory Board for the Research Councils. In 1982 the Board concluded that 'the blame must fall primarily on the universities rather than on the research students'.

A major cause of these failures is the poor standard of supervision offered to many post-graduate students. The universities are anxious however not to publicise their own failings, and departments do not publish failure and non-completion rates. A working party of the British Psychological Society (BPS) recently investigated the views of Psychology Department Heads and research students on post-graduate education in psychology. In 1983 they reported that fourteen out of thirty-nine Department Heads regarded the present system as 'clearly unsatisfactory' referring most frequently to poor supervision 'either because the supervisor was too laissez-faire or was incompetent'. Such findings are not always welcome in academic circles: although a summary of the BPS report has been published, the full document has been suppressed.

Anne Hawkins and Peter Hawkins of RULES (Reform University Law and Educational Standards) have identified a number of characteristic features typically associated with postgraduate students who believe their work has been unfairly rejected. These are summarised below.

1.   The student is not told why the work has been rejected. Material evidence such as the reports of supervisors and examiners, or examination marks, are withheld.
The following extracts are from letters received by former students whose cases have been taken up by RULES:

> You enquire about your rights to obtain information about the examiners' assessments. As a candidate for a degree you are not able to see the examiners' reports which are normally circulated in confidence to members of the Board of the Faculty.

> I am afraid that the University's 'Instructions to Examiners' are a matter for the Examiners and the University alone and I do not feel able to send the complete sheet to you.

> There is no document prescribing procedures. There are procedures, there is no Procedure.
> (Extracts from letters (1982–83) from Hull University to a PhD candidate whose thesis had been rejected.)

> It is not possible to let you see the reports of the Examiners on your thesis: these reports are made by Examiners on the understanding that they are confidential to the University and candidates have no right to see such reports.
> (Letter from the Vice Chancellor of Manchester University (18.1.84) to Edward Black in connection with his rejected MA thesis.)

> You ask in your letter for a copy of the examiners reports. These are confidential and cannot be divulged to candidates.
> (Letter from the Registrar of Hull University (8.2.82) to Alistair Wilson in connection with his rejected PhD thesis.)

2.   Even information about appeal procedures may be difficult to obtain.
A recent examination of thirty-one different university calendars plus a number from some of their constituent colleges revealed that only one contained a procedure for appealing against a decision of the board of examiners. Some universities have no formal appeals procedure at all: students may have no way of knowing how to submit an appeal, what grounds for appeal will be considered, or who will hear it.

A student who in March 1982 appealed against the rejection of her PhD thesis by Hull University had her appeal heard by a specially appointed 'ad hoc' committee. The student was not told that the Senate meeting which had set up this 'ad hoc' committee on 5 May had, earlier in the same session, approved a wholly separate new formal Postgraduate Review Procedure. The new procedure should have allowed the student to present her case to a properly constituted appeal committee in person – an opportunity in fact denied to her.

Yet the Vice-Chancellor repeatedly assured her that the 'approved procedures' had been followed. She has still been denied information about the composition and terms of reference of the improperly constituted committee which heard her appeal. Moreover, she later learnt that part of her complaint had not been considered by this committee although the university did not inform her of this. She has been told she may re-appeal under the formal review procedure but, a year later, has still not been told what criteria it will adopt. According to the university, 'The procedure for the (appeal) committee will be a matter for that committee.'

3.   *The student is not permitted to question the academic judgement of his examiners.*

For example, London's Imperial College Regulations state that students who are asked to withdraw through failure to maintain satisfactory academic progress have 'the right to appeal against the withdrawal decision but not against the results of any examination or academic assessment on which the decision might be based'. This would successfully negate most appeals that might be made on the grounds of examiners' error, negligence or inappropriate fields of speciality.

At CSE examinations and 'O' and 'A' levels a parent or the school can ask not only to have a particular paper re-marked, but also to have a report supplied to them outlining how the marks were allocated in a particular candidate's paper. It is also standard university practice to moderate their examinations for lower awards – though this also may be done in a secretive manner. However, there is no equivalent procedure for PhD examinations.

4.   *There is no provision for the independent academic assessment of a thesis subject to appeal.*

A student who is seriously aggrieved at a university's handling of his appeal can turn to the University's Visitor. In most cases the Visitor is technically the Queen, though complaints would in practice be handled by the Privy Council. Letters from the Privy Council suggest that it will not normally question a university's academic assessment and will intervene only if the university has failed to adhere to its own procedures.

5.   *A student whose supervisor is also a senior faculty member may find it extremely difficult to complain effectively if he believes he has been inadequately supervised.*

A London University student whose MA thesis was rejected in 1980 found that his supervisor, Head of Department, and Chairman of the Board of Examiners were all one and the same person – and that his professor was also initially responsible for handling the student's appeal.

The student has pointed out that before submitting the thesis he asked the professor – in his role as supervisor – whether he had reservations about the quality of the dissertation. He argues that, if the thesis genuinely was substandard it was the professor's duty – as his supervisor – to inform him of this, giving him the opportunity to improve it and delay submission to a later date.

6.   *There may sometimes be grounds for supposing that an examiner may be biased against a student – yet it is extremely difficult to obtain a re-examination even under such circumstances.*

In presenting original work – often a requirement for a higher degree – it may be necessary for a student to criticise some conflicting schools of thought. It is impossible to justify the appointment as examiner of anyone from such a conflicting school, since the examiner's work may be criticised in the thesis.

In 1983 the supervisor of a London University PhD candidate refused to endorse the appointment of the proposed external examiner, pointing out that the nominee 'is the least suitable candidate as an external examiner for (the student) . . . in his forthcoming (publication) . . . he has unreservedly accepted . . . all the results . . . which are very severely (and in the view of very many scholars, including me, fully convincingly) criticised by . . . (the student). I cannot imagine a more unsuitable choice of external examiner'.

7.   *A student whose thesis has been rejected is unable to resubmit the same thesis, even after making modifications.*

University rules also explicitly prevent a student submitting a failed thesis to a different university, where he feels he may obtain an independent evaluation of his work.

A university is contractually bound to provide certain educational services to the students it accepts. If the student suggests that the university may be in breach of contract, then the university administration owes him a duty to deal with his complaints fairly and openly. At present, universities are free to use their considerable autonomy, their control over academic records, assessments and other information, to cover-up their own shortcomings.

Some of the examples described here breach fundamental principles of law; that no-one may be a judge in his own cause; that both sides of the case shall be heard; and that the participant should have the right to know the opposing case.

Ironically, a student who wishes to appeal against a *disciplinary* decision may have these rights. He can see evidence, call and cross-examine witnesses, and if necessary obtain a public hearing with legal representation in order to appeal against a fine for, say, parking his bike on the university lawn.

Examiners who cannot examine publicly, and are not prepared to defend their assessments, are not worthy to be appointed examiners. Under present arrangements, they are in a position to make decisions that can seriously damage the lives of students while being unwilling to risk their own reputations by openly justifying their decisions.

Students whose theses are rejected after several years' of intensive work are generally very vulnerable. It is not unusual to find them suffering profound feelings of guilt, rejection and isolation. It is a gross dereliction of the university's responsibilities if it does not help that student appreciate why his work was found wanting, ensure on his behalf that the decision was indeed justified, and help the student to build positively on those aspects of his work that can be salvaged.

RULES wants universities to be publicly accountable for their academic performance. It is pressing for students to be given a right of access to academic and other evaluations about them, and the right to comment on and if necessary appeal against them to an open, independent and effective forum. It is also pressing for fair treatment for those individuals cited here who have become casualties of university secrecy as well as for many others similarly affected.

Medical records

In May 1983, an inter-professional working group serviced by the British Medical Association reported in favour of greater access by patients to information about their health:

> We support the right of patients and clients to have access to all information which is held about them on their behalf. Such access encourages openness and can improve the quality of the record by correcting factual errors and reducing misunderstandings.

The working group, however, qualified its general support arguing that:

> there are some situations in which the unregulated release of the entire clinical or social record could cause distress, or even harm, to a patient or client, or to someone else. In some cases, the personal record may also include information on others who are entitled to have their confidences kept. Also, many records

would be unintelligible to a layman without professional interpretation and explanation.

It went on to suggest that for these reasons the extent of disclosure should be left to the discretion of the doctor concerned – with an appeal procedure for those who might not be satisfied:

> the imposition of an *absolute* requirement to afford unrestriced access could inhibit health professionals from recording sensitive information or opinions to the inevitable detriment of patient care: an acceptable mechanism must therefore be devised for the exercise of a proper discretion by the responsible clinician or other health professional. This should provide for subject access to the extent and in the manner judged most helpful by the responsible clinician or an appropriate colleague. Any subject who is dissatisfied with this arrangement should then have a right to seek access through an independent health professional of his choice, practising in the same discipline or speciality as the responsible clinician or other health professional. There may in the last resort remain a legal right to seek access to information which has still been withheld. It would be appropriate for such a right to be exercised through the courts, which could decide the issue. We believe that this would arise only exceptionally.

Under the contracts of service which GPs make with the National Health Service they are obliged to keep adequate records of the illnesses and treatment of their patients on forms supplied by the Family Practitioner Committees. Technically, these records belong to the DHSS, while the records of privately treated patients belong to the doctor or hospital involved. But, unlike a solicitor's files – which technically belong to the client – the patient does not own his or her medical records.

The question of ownership is not merely a technicality. The Community Rights Project has collected details of a number of cases in which patients have been, quite unreasonably, denied access to records which 'belong' not to them but to the health service. Take, for instance, the following case:

> In January 1984, Mrs Janey Tucker wrote to the Greater Glasgow Health Board explaining that she and her family expected to leave Britain in the near future to settle permanently in another country. She asked whether her and her family's medical records could be sent to her new doctor in Holland when they had registered there.
>
> She was told that (a) the records were confidential and the private property of the NHS (b) there was no mechanism for transferring such records abroad (c) the only records she could have from her NHS file were any that might originally have come from other countries where she may privately have paid for treatment (d) if her doctor in her new country required information he should write to her former GP who would be free to consult the NHS records held by the Board before replying, and (e) her NHS records would be retained by the Health Board for a period of three years and, if the family had not returned by then, destroyed.

If these are the problems which face a patient who merely wishes to transfer her records to a new doctor, it is not hard to imagine the difficulties faced by a patient who wants the record in order to substantiate a claim of negligence. If a case comes to court – or is likely to – the litigant can seek disclosure under Section 32 of the Administration of Justice Act 1970. A DHSS circular suggests that hospitals should anticipate the likely views of the courts in deciding whether to release such information – an attitude which suggests that disclosure may take place only when there is already evidence of negligence:

> Where a request for records or reports is made on what are manifestly insubstantial grounds, the hospital cannot be expected to grant it, but where information is being sought in pursuance of a claim of prima facie substance against the Board or Committee or a member of their staff or both, the decision is more difficult and each request must be examined on its own merits, in the light of legal advice, and of course in consultation with any member of their medical or dental staff directly concerned in the outcome of the claim . . . The production of case notes and similar documents is not obligatory before the stage of discovery in the actual proceedings is reached, but the Minister does not feel that Boards and Committees, especially as they are public authorities, would either wish to be well advised to maintain their strict rights in this connection except for some good reason . . .
>
> (Circular HM (59) (88))

Following the Supreme Court Act 1981 the DHSS has issued a further circular, again advising health authorities not to resist disclosure in situations where the High Court would be likely to require it:

> In cases of doubt account should continue to be taken of the powers of the High Court to order disclosure in advance of proceedings. It would not be appropriate for health authorities to adopt a more stringent test than would be likely to be applied by the court . . . since this could have the effect of forcing the applicant to resort to court action when there was no real doubt as to the outcome.

This circular does to some extent suggest a slight relaxation of the criteria to be met before records are disclosed. It points out that a court does not need to be convinced of the merit of an applicant's claim before it will order disclosure, *merely that there are reasonable grounds for taking action*. The Community Rights Project points out that even so, patients may still be unable to obtain details of their medical treatment:

> It is clear that many patients still find themselves going through the courts merely to secure notes, before they and their legal/medical advisers can determine if they have a strong or even viable case. This acts as a real discouragement to patients pursuing a claim.

It is not only in the relatively rare cases where complaints of negligence or malpractice occur that patients may want access to their medical records. According to Dame Elizabeth Ackroyd of the Patients Association:

> the problems arise when the patient is suspicious that the notes include comments about him which reflect the doctor's subjective view of him – his personality and behaviour – which goes outside his medical condition. This would not matter so much perhaps if only the doctor in question kept the notes. But they are part of the patient's medical baggage which follows him around. Under the NHS if you change your GP . . . the medical records are transferred to your new doctor. If you are referred for hospital treatment relevant parts of your notes will follow you in and out.

Such subjective views, if they occur on a medical record, may acquire a quite unmerited authority. According to Dr D. F. H. Pheby:

> because of the prestige of the medical profession, medical diagnosis in . . . (behavioural) fields also are often treated as objective conclusions from scientific facts, even though they contain a substantial judgemental element . . . The labelled patient who is late for his appointment is 'irresponsible', while the patient who is early or on time is 'obsessional' . . . How many parents have been told by health professionals of various types that their child is 'hyperactive' when what is really meant is 'busy'?
>
> (*Journal of Medical Ethics*, 1982, 8, 12–24)

Once patients are 'labelled' in their medical notes it may be impossible for them to remove what may be a highly subjective but very damaging entry:

> In January 1982 a young woman secured a number of interviews for good secretarial posts. The offers of appointment, however, were accompanied by a medical certificate with a request that she should ask her GP to complete it and return it to the company. She then realised that several offers of employment had been withdrawn after prospective employers had received their certificates.
>
> She learnt from her GP that he has stated on the form that she suffers from 'anxiety neurosis' – but he is not prepared to discuss the matter with her. The only justification she could see for the remark is that some years ago, when a teenager, she was referred to a consultant psychiatrist for consultation. She made one or two visits to the consultant as an outpatient, but was never admitted to any psychiatric hospital, and the consultant eventually said that she did not suffer any psychiatric problem. As a result of her employment difficulties she has again made contact with the consultant who has told her she thinks it most unreasonable of the GP to have entered the phrase 'anxiety neurosis' on any medical certificate. That comment – which is presumably entered on her medical records – may nevertheless follow her round for the rest of her life. There is no formal procedure whereby a patient can directly apply for an amendment to be made in his or her medical records.

The Patients Association has described other cases where the people concerned know, or suspect, that there is a mistaken diagnosis in their records which is damaging to them in a variety of ways.

> A girl was wrongly diagnosed as a chronic schizophrenic. Subsequently her parents were told that this diagnosis was incorrect and that it would be expunged from the records. However, this evidently was not done and the girl's subsequent medical treatment was dogged by this damaging label – she was given inappropriate drugs and there was difficulty in getting a GP to accept her. The mother (Mrs K E) said 'We have been literally hounded by various GPs because we have had the temerity to complain and to contest a diagnosis, and we are "blacklisted"'.

In this case the people concerned became aware of what was in the records. In most of the cases brought to the Patients Association they only suspect what is in their records and resent the fact that they cannot see and perhaps challenge comments which appear to be damaging their lives in some ways.

The question of patient access to records raises another related issue: who else sees these records, and if they contain subjective judgements mixed in with diagnosis, could these prejudice the decisions that others are taking?

The Community Rights Project has suggested that the list of those with direct access to a hospital patient's medical records apart from doctors and consultants may include nurses, hospital pharmacy staff, radiologists, medical social workers, health visitors, midwives, technicians, filing clerks, administrative personnel and even porters (who may carry the records, along with the patient). In addition, information from the medical records may be widely circulated elsewhere, particularly if the patient is the subject of an interdisciplinary 'case conference'. Thus information may reach social workers, probation officers, education welfare officers, teachers, the juvenile court and the police.

Dr Pheby's comments on the dangers of unscientific medical labelling are most relevant here:

> At case conferences concerned with alleged cases of child abuse, it is by no means unusual for only a small minority of those present to have any direct personal knowledge of either the child or the family. The majority are therefore unable to judge for themselves the quality of the evidence on which they are basing their conclusions. Information is tossed back and forth between professionals of different disciplines who form judgements on it and pass it on with their own views appended, so that eventually a remarkably united consensus may be achieved by the multi-disciplinary team, the members of which can then quote each other in corroboration of their views. However, underlying the whole edifice may be one single medical pronouncement about some behavioural phenomenon which, being basically unscientific, can never be falsified.

Moreover, there are other bodies – such as employers or insurance companies – who may insist on being allowed to take up medical references on those who apply to them. Once patients are 'labelled' in their medical notes it may be impossible for them to remove or correct what may be highly subjective, or inaccurate and extremely damaging entries about them.

Mental health records

It is perhaps in the area of psychiatric illness that the need for patients to be able to see their own medical records becomes most acute. Many kinds of illness have serious consequences, but it is only the patient who is judged to be suffering from psychiatric illness who may be locked up in hospital against his will or treated without his consent. Moreover, the former psychiatric patient often suffers from serious discrimination when trying to find employment. In 1978, MIND documented forty such cases in its report 'Nobody Wants You'. In such cases crucial employment decisions may be taken on the basis of confidential medical reports which the individual is unable to see or challenge, as the following examples show. The first concerns a student nurse:

[She] had a nervous breakdown and was admitted to hospital six months after starting her training. She was fit to return after two months, but it was suggested she take a further month's sick leave. While on this leave, she was asked to attend the occupational health department for a medical examination, though no reasons for this were advanced. Five days later she received a letter terminating her training. She appealed against this decision submitting evidence from her own psychiatrist that she was entirely fit to return to work. *The report from the occupational health department was not shown to her representative at the hearing and her dismissal was upheld.*

After a nervous breakdown and a period of time in hospital he (an assistant museum keeper) was compulsorily retired on medical grounds – with only a week's notice. He subsequently discovered that the treasury medical officer had decided on his retirement against his psychiatrist's advice. He then spent a year trying to get another job and finally became a librarian in a local library where he has remained for the past sixteen years. His medical record has prevented him from returning to specialised museum work.

In 1977 after an argument in the street – which led to the police being called – Buddy Larrier was forcibly taken to a hospital casualty department and, despite his objections, given an injection. He woke up the next day in another hospital where, he learnt, he had been placed under Section 25 of the 1959 Mental Health Act, which enables patients suffering from mental disorder to be compulsorily detained for up to twenty-eight days. After his discharge he lost the job he had held for the previous ten years – as a bus driver with London Transport – and his public service vehicle driving licence.

Mr Larrier had no history of mental illness. He has been told that he was admitted having been diagnosed as psychotic and possibly suffering from schizophrenia – a diagnosis he rejects. He has never been allowed to see the admission forms or medical assessments that led to his enforced hospital admission. The Greenwich and Bexley Area Health Authority has stated: 'It is not our general practice to release copies of the applications under sections of the Mental Health Act or of the medical recommendations supporting them as they are regarded as part of the patient's medical record.'

In some of these examples the individuals involved had independent evidence to suggest that they were capable of carrying on what they had been denied – their normal employment. But the argument here is not primarily whether the original diagnosis or decision was right, but whether everything possible to *ensure* that it would be right had been done.

Medical records like any others may contain information that is out-of-date or inaccurate, or opinion that is unsubstantiated. Where mental health is involved, such information could jeopardise not only the treatment, but also the employment, future livelihood and even liberty of those involved. We can reasonably expect the maximum safeguards against the wrong decisions being taken in such circumstances; without the right to see and correct the medical record, such safeguards cannot exist.

The benefits of disclosure

Allowing patients access to their medical notes would not only provide a safeguard against error: it could also make a direct positive contribution to the relationship between the patient and doctor, and the patient's involvement in the treatment.

The withholding of files implies that the patient is a passive participant in the treatment process who is unable to understand or face the reality of his condition. Of course, the medical record may not be wholly intelligible to the lay reader: but the process of asking questions and making sense of the answers may be a crucial step in helping the patient assume a greater share of the responsibility for his or her own health.

Patients frequently complain that they are poorly informed about their medical condition and treatment. It is common for one in three patients to express dissatisfaction, and in some surveys as many as two thirds of those asked have been unhappy with the information provided.

A 1982 review of research on patient access to information concluded that 'It would appear from survey evidence that the majority of patients wish to know as much as possible about their illness, its causes, its treatment, and its outcome.' It added that 'patients probably want to know more about their medication than the professionals would wish to tell them'. For example, one US survey found that 77 per cent of patients – but only 25 per cent of doctors – felt that patients should be told 'all possible risks of normal use' of their medication (Philip Ley, 'Giving Information to Patients' in J. R. Eiser (ed), *Social Psychology and Behavioural Medicine*, Wiley, 1982).

On the other hand, where access to medical records has been given, considerable benefits have been found. At St Thomas' Hospital, London pregnant women are given charge of their health records: they are asked to keep them at home and bring them with them to every appointment. Some doctors initially feared that records would be forgotten or lost. In fact, in the several years that the scheme has operated not a single woman has given birth without her records present. Previously, between three and five deliveries *a week* took place without staff having the records at hand.

Patients in a small medical centre in the state of Vermont, USA, have since 1972 been given a full set of their records on admission. A survey of how a group of about 100 of them reacted was published in 1976: although 60 per cent asked questions about the vocabulary or meaning of terms they often 'expressed a sense of relief at having the secrecy removed from their records and were pleasantly surprised to be treated as adults'. Doctors from the centre reported:

Patients who were in a stage of denial simply sorted out for themselves what they could deal with at the time and gave the staff adequate guidelines as to where they should stop. It was helpful for each team member to know that the patient already had access to everything in the record. There needed to be no hesitation based on 'I don't know what he has been told' . . . The admission note at the bedside became a central point in patient–team interaction . . . The patients used their records to explain themselves to their families . . . Most patients reacted positively to the receipt of the written record. Some patients chose not to deal with the record . . . perhaps preferring not to accept the responsibility of knowing. We could identify no instance in which a patient was harmed by being offered his record . . . The fact that the report was a carbon copy of the hospital record was interpreted as a declaration of openness and trust.

(*Arch. Phys. Med. Rehabil.* 57, Feb. 1976, 78–81)

The same report noted how patients contributed to their records: '50 per cent made some addition or correction on a point of fact' as they read their notes. Given the poor state of the records in some NHS hospitals such an input from patients would be invaluable. A 1983 survey of the records kept in two hospitals in Wales found that admission records described patients' initial treatment in only 16 per cent of cases; a quarter of them failed to record the patients' principal complaints; nearly a half omitted the allergy history; and three-quarters of the X-rays carried out were not reported in the case notes (*Journal of the Royal College of Physicians*, 17 (3), July 1983, 208–212).

Social work

The decisions that social workers are required to take or contribute to can have critical effects on the lives of those involved. Children may be removed from their parents, young people may be given custodial sentences, the old placed in institutions, the psychiatrically ill compulsorily admitted to hospital, while welfare benefits or housing may be obtained or lost – all on the basis of information kept on social service departments' files.

For some, such as children admitted into care at an early age, the files are not only the basis for crucial decisions about their lives, they are also a record of their lives, the one source of continuous information about background or personal history. The comments of young people in care about the way in which decisions about them are taken and recorded are particularly relevant in any discussion about social work files.

By law, the position of every young person in care must be reviewed every six months. If everything is going well the review may consist of a meeting between the social worker and his or her supervisor. But if there are problems – or likely to be some change in the young person's circumstances – a 'case conference', perhaps involving many more people may be held. According to the National Association of Young People in Care (NAYPIC):

> it often appears to young people that the more problems there are the more strange people turn up at a review. Young people seldom have any say in who attends their review and they are often surprised and upset when they see how many apparent strangers will hear about the often painful and difficult details of their lives . . . Often young people choose not to attend their review because they feel outnumbered, they do not know the other people and do not believe what they have to say will really be listened to.
>
> (*Sharing Care*, NAYPIC, 1983)

A survey of 465 young people in childrens' homes or foster care in 1983 found that less than a third saw the written reports considered at their reviews. Less than a quarter had the chance to write and submit their own report to a review – though two thirds of the young people said they would have liked to do this (*Gizza Say: Reviews and Young People in Care*, M. Stein and S. Ellis, NAYPIC, 1983).

It is not only those in care who may feel deprived of this information. As in the next case described, those *offering* care are also the subject of social workers' files.

In January 1983 a local authority social services department removed two children from the family which had fostered them for the previous nine months. The children had originally been placed there as a temporary measure, but the foster parents found that they were happy and when a possible move was suggested offered to provide them with a permanent home. The social services department clearly felt this would not be a suitable arrangement – but have never offered what the foster parents find a convincing reason why. According to the foster mother:

> They claim they have proof the children were not happy and settled with us, despite the fact that the neighbours and everyone around here says that they were. Well, let's have a look at it and see if its true. We don't mind if it's hurtful to us. We couldn't imagine that our lives were so bad that they had to remove the children from us and place them in an institution.

Finally, at 24 hours notice, the children were moved to a children's home and subsequently to another family.

The foster parents have never been told what led to this decision – and have been refused access to the file about them held by the social services department.

> We were never allowed to say anything or clarify any points or defend ourselves . . . Comments about our life style and family and even remarks which we have made have been distorted, misrepresented and in some cases are untruthful. These remain on the (children's) or our file and were presumably used as evidence for the Social Services Department's decisions. We feel we are entitled to see what has been written about us and be given a chance to correct any misrepresentations.

The third corner of this triangle are the parents of children whom the local authority believes may be at risk in their own homes. Social services departments keep 'child abuse registers' where the names of such children are entered. The DHSS encourages local authorities to inform the parents when a child's name is placed on this register, though according to the Family Rights Group this is not always done. Parents in such situations may be under great stress, and welcome offers of support and counselling from the local authority. In some cases they may not know that the local authority is worried about the safety of their children and, perhaps, considering a care order. Equally, there may be times when the local authority's concern is in fact not justified, but the parent who does not know of it has no opportunity to set the record straight.

The DHSS in a 1983 consultation paper on disclosure of social workers' files acknowledges that the information held on them cannot always be strictly factual: 'It is also sometimes of great importance to include impressions and opinions which are of crucial significance . . . in enabling accurate assessments to be made.' Inevitably the danger is that extremely subjective opinions will become bound up with professional assessments. John Taylor, a team worker in Barnsley Social Services has written:

I have seen the evidence for myself in educational, medical and social work practice – that people who have professional positions do make entries on files for which there is little or no evidence, entries which are personally offensive because untrue, entries which say more about that worker's insecurity or personal inadequacy than they do about the person to whom they refer.

(Letter to *Community Care* magazine, 30.9.82)

The Chidren's Legal Centre has described a case which took place in 1980 when a London council was asked to remove the parental rights of a mother of three children:

It was discovered that the social worker's file contained information about another mother with the same name, but with four children. When asked how such a mistake could have occurred, given the difference in numbers of children, the social workers said that they thought the mother was 'denying' the existence of her fourth child.

At least the *principle* of allowing social workers 'clients' the right to see their own files has now been widely acknowledged. In 1983 the British Association of Social Workers itself called for an opening of social work files:

Individuals should have a right (subject to any legal restrictions) to see and copy personal information held about them. We believe that the practical difficulties of allowing clients to have access to their case records are less than they may at first sight seem. Given this, we consider that preventing clients from having access to their case records is unnecessarily restrictive. It can not be justified consistently because there are many cases where all would agree that no harm would result from the client having access to the case record. Even where some information contained in the case record should not be disclosed to the client, this does not mean that all the information contained in the record should be kept from the client. To follow the ideas we have already outlined we believe that client access should be the norm and not the exception . . .

Individuals should have the right to challenge, correct and amend personal information recorded about them. Given that clients should have access to their case records we see no practical difficulties in their having the right to amend personal information recorded about them where this is clearly incorrect or a matter of unsupported conjecture on the part of the social worker.

Social workers and agencies should see access to and involvement in writing and correcting records as an integral part of the social work process. This would enhance trust and equality between client and social worker and helps social work intervention to be more effective because it is better understood by all parties to it . . .

('Effective and Ethical Recording. Report of the Case Recording & Group', BASW, 1983)

A Department of Health and Social Security circular issued in August 1983 also supports the principle of open access – though in this case subject to major qualifications:

> The Secretary of State shares the increasingly held view that people receiving personal social services should, subject to adequate safeguards be able to discuss what is said about them in social services records. It has always been good practice for social services staff to share non-confidential information with clients in the context of an open professional relationship and this approach will and should continue. But in the past, case records have been regarded as private, internal documents and have been compiled on the basis that their contents would never be disclosed. *The Secretary of State's view is that in future – with a number of necessary exceptions – those clients who wish to have access to written records should be allowed to do so* . . . (emphasis added)
> (Circular LAC(83) 14)

However, the circular goes on to state that in certain exceptional circumstances disclosure might be harmful and should not take place. Some of these exceptions are reasonable, but others are unnecessarily – and unacceptably – wide. The DHSS comments together with the responses to them of Rachel Hodgkin and Jenny Kuper of the Children's Legal Centre (CLC) are shown below:

1. Protecting third parties

The Circular states: 'A client's record may include information about a third party which, whether given in confidence or not, could if disclosed to the client harm the third party by damaging his reputation or relationship. For example a child's record may include information about his paternity given by the child's mother. Moreover third parties have rights to privacy which should not be subordinated to the client's right of access.'

CLC comments that it is true that social work files often contain information about another person which is relevant to social work with the client. But difficulties arising from this can be minimised, if not eradicated, by ensuring that separate files are kept for each client – for example, family files should not exist – and that irrelevant or out-of-date information is excluded. The British Association of Social Workers (BASW) sets out, in *Effective and Ethical Recording: Report of the BASW Case Recording Project Group*, certain principles along these lines, and further provide that: 'Records of activities or behaviour which have relevance to more than one individual should be treated as personal information and kept on the files of all individuals to which they apply.' However if information about third parties is relevant and should be on the file, then the client has a right to see it – no matter how 'difficult' the information is. As social work files are by and large about relationships between people, to withhold this information would make 'subject access' a nonsense.

2. Protecting sources of information

The Circular states: 'Policies for community care depend on the cooperation of . . . sources – on collaboration between professions and agencies, and in enlisting friends and neighbours in informal networks of interest and support. To provide an effective service it is important that social services departments should continue to receive information from all these sources . . . [who] should feel free to speak candidly and should not be inhibited by the knowledge that their identity or the information they provide might be disclosed to the person concerned, or used for a purpose other than that for which it was supplied.'

CLC comments that there is some strength in the argument that someone who is not acting in a professional capacity should be able to give information to social services but request that their identity be kept a secret. However, in the interests of justice, the client should have access to the information itself – in order, if necessary to challenge it or participate in the full investigation of it. A model for this approach already exists in the United States: in cases of suspected child abuse, the New York City Department of Social Services always informs parents of allegations (excepting the informant's identity) and gives them the opportunity to request a fair hearing to 'expunge, seal or amend' the entry on their file. As regards *professional* sources of information (e.g. medical or police reports) there is no reason why both the information and the identity of the informant should not be disclosed.

3. Protecting social workers' confidential judgements

The Circular states: 'Social workers may find it necessary in the long-term interests of both children and adults to commit tentative opinions and observations to paper. Social workers and other social services department staff cannot and should not form snap judgements and may find it necessary to make recorded entries before opinions and subsequent decisions can be made. Furthermore, the inevitable movement of staff means that, if the interests of those cared for are to be served, full written information needs to be available on file in order to provide continuity in good professional practice. There should not be a secondary system to covert records.'

CLC comments that although social workers do from time to time need to make confidential judgements these should not be made or kept on the personal file of clients, where – particularly because of the inevitable movement of staff – judgements are liable to be misread or misused by others who have access to the file. BASW's recommendations support this view: 'Agencies should have a system for ensuring that social workers have means of thinking about and planning their work, but agency records should not be used for this purpose', and: 'Conjectures about clients' circumstances or personalities should be restricted to social workers' private notes and should not form part of the agency record.'

Social workers should of course be able to keep private notes (how could one stop them?), but these should *not* form 'a secondary system of covert records'. Private notes should be strictly personal aide memoires, kept only when necessary for the *personal* use of the social worker and not transferred to the client's file or shown to anyone else. If such private notes were to be transferred to the file then they would become part of the file and should be subject to full client access.

4. Children and parents

The Circular states: 'Parents' (or guardians') absolute right of access to records about their children would ignore the fact that the interests of parent and child may be separate and may conflict. Many children are in care because of a breakdown in relationship with their parents, or because of inadequate parental care and this may be reflected in the records in terms that the parent may be unable to accept. The child (who may be as old as eighteen) may not want the parent to see the record. The local authority is under a duty . . . to ascertain the child's wishes about any decision affecting him and to give due consideration to these wishes taking account of his age and understanding. It also states: 'requests from children or young people should be treated in the same way as requests from adults. Sensitive information about a child in the records should not be given to the parents without the child's consent, unless the child is precluded by reason of age or mental disorder from understanding the full significance of the information and thus of giving an informed consent.'

CLC comments that conflicts of interest between parent and child are a legitimate concern, and by and large the Circular deals sensibly with the complicated issue of children's rights. It is appropriate to withhold from a parent information that the child may not want disclosed. However, if the child consents to the disclosure, parents have a legitimate right to the information – it should not be withheld because a social worker believes the parent may be 'unable to accept' it.

5. Protecting the client

The Circular states: 'There may be some cases where a person receiving services would be harmed by knowing the facts about himself in his case records that may be disturbing, even if given to him by professional staff e.g. an elderly person may learn he is less than welcome to his family, a child may learn his parents have a criminal record or history of mental disorder. Among people referred to social services departments are those disturbed emotionally and even comparatively mundane matters recorded about them may have, to them, a special and damaging significance. An aim of social work is to enable people to come to terms with such facts but this needs care and sometimes prolonged counselling, and will not always succeed. A minority who are unstable or have little insight, may need to be protected permanently from certain damaging revelations.'

CLC comments that this is an extremely dangerous category on which to permit non-disclosure, as it rests entirely on the judgement of the 'professionals' as to whether refusing access would protect the client or not. Once the client knows of the existence of the file and persists in wanting to see it it is very difficult to see how the professional could convince the client that access would not be in his or her best interests. Clients may of course need careful counselling before or when upsetting information is revealed. But to deny them information they know exists on the grounds that secrecy is in their own interests may often be as, or more, disturbing than the information itself.

These arguments were previously submitted to the DHSS by a group of organisations, including the Children's Legal Centre, the Campaign for Mentally Handicapped People, the Association for Disabled Professionals, the Family Rights Group, the National Council for One Parent Families, MIND, the Advisory Centre for Education, the Campaign for the Advancement of State Education, and the National Council for Civil Liberties. They did not prevail, and social workers are now guided by a government Circular which, in effect, could prevent the disclosure of every social work file in the country.

Opening the files

The Data Protection Bill
Some – very limited – access to personal records will be possible in the future when the Data Protection Bill becomes law. The following description refers to the Bill as it stands at the time of writing (Spring 1984) though it is possible that some changes may be introduced before it becomes law.

The Bill proposes that any information held on computer about an identifiable person will be protected in accordance with a number of principles. The information should be:

- held and used only for specified lawful purposes;
- adequate and relevant – but not excessive – for the purpose;
- accurate and, where necessary, kept up-to-date and not retained after it is no longer necessary;
- properly protected by security measures against unauthorised access or disclosure, and against loss, alteration or destruction;
- open to inspection by the subjects of the information, who may have inaccurate or irrelevant information corrected or removed.

Those who hold information about individuals on computers must be properly registered: they can be barred from keeping or processing personal data on computers if they fail to comply with the data protection principles.

A public register of data users will be kept. Members of the public can consult this free of charge to find out who is holding and using computerised personal information and to whom it may be lawfully disclosed. They can then contact the holder of the information and find out whether information about themselves is included.

The Bill proposes to give individuals a right or access to computerised information about themselves on payment of a (so far unspecified) fee. It will also give them the right to see the information and correct it if it is inaccurate. They will be able to enforce these rights in the courts and obtain compensation for damage caused by inaccurate or misleading information.

Exemptions

This is fine as far as it goes, but the principles of the Bill are subject to a number of far-reaching and fundamental exemptions. Because of these, the Bill may give little consolation to many people faced with the kinds of problems described in this chapter.

The Bill will not cover ordinary, non-computerised records.

Handwritten or typed notes stored on record cards or in files are totally exempt from the Bill. Most of the records described in this chapter will be stored on paper rather than computer. Individuals will have no right to see or correct such records, and no right of remedy if they are used for unauthorised purposes.

There may be restricted access to some of the more important computerised systems of information.

The Bill gives the Home Secretary the power to exempt from subject access information from health or social work records and other data which he believes ought to remain confidential. Additionally, individuals will have no right of access to information about themselves where this is thought likely to prejudice the prevention or detection of crime or the assessment and collection of any tax or duty.

Why should a data protection law *allow* such anomalies, if its object really is to protect the rights of people about whom records are kept?

The short answer is that the Bill has not been introduced primarily to protect the rights of the individual – but to protect industry. Many countries now have their own data protection laws – and these prohibit the transfer of information to countries, such as the UK, which do not have similar laws. British companies operating abroad, and the British computer industry, would be seriously disadvantaged unless legislation that at least meets a minimum standard is introduced. Without such legislation, a multinational company which had linked up its computers over much of the world would have to exclude its British subsidiary from the network. Equally, British data processing firms would be unable to compete for overseas business. It is such considerations, rather than the problems of those about whom records are kept, that have prompted and shaped the Data Protection Bill.

What happens abroad?
Other countries have gone already much further than Britain is now proposing to go in opening up records to their subjects. In the United States, the Freedom of Information Act allows individuals to obtain records held about them by federal agencies. However, they frequently apply for such information under the 1974 Privacy Act – which gives them the additional power to correct inaccuracies they may find.

The Privacy Act requires federal agencies to publicly identify all systems of records maintained on individuals. It places a legal duty on them to ensure that the information in these records is accurate, complete, relevant and up-to-date and allows individuals to inspect the data held about them and correct inaccuracies. Agencies must keep records of who has been allowed access to such information, and make this list of disclosures available to the subject of the information. The individual's consent is required before an agency can use information collected for one purpose for any other reason.

There are a number of specific exemptions to subject access – for example, documents concerning national defence, criminal law enforcement, or the work of the Secret Service, while there are much wider exemptions for records held by the CIA or FBI. However, agencies do not always insist on their right to withhold exempted information. In 1981 the CIA disclosed at least some information from exempted records to 30 per cent of requesters. Such information sometimes includes even reports of security agents, though with informants' names deleted.

The Privacy and Freedom of Information Acts refer only to federal records – but access to some other records is possible under separate legislation. The 1974 Family Educational Rights and Privacy Act provides a right to pupil records at schools and colleges receiving federal funds.

The Act gives parents rights (which transfer to the student at the age of eighteen) to see records held by schools and ask them to correct inaccurate information. If necessary, they have the right to a formal hearing under an independent chairman and if the school still does not agree to correct the record they can enter a note on the files expressing their concerns.

Schools can normally release information from a pupil's records only to certain specified bodies – for example, a school to which the pupil is transferring, the source of the pupil's grant, or certain government officials. Disclosure to others – including the police, probation service or employers – may not take place without the permission of the parents or student, who also can demand to see school or college references written about them.

In at least twenty-four states in the USA separate legislations allows access to medical records.

Freedom of Information laws in Australia, Canada and New Zealand also allow individuals to see information about themselves on federal government files. In 1983 the first annual report on Australia's new Freedom of Information Act showed that a total of 3,352 requests (more than half of all under the Act) were to the Departments of Social Security, Veterans' Affairs and Taxation, agencies where record-keeping is a major function.

Some European countries – Denmark, France, Norway and Sweden – also allow access to personal information under freedom of information type legislation. Such rights also exist under data protection legislation. Such laws, or administrative practice under them, in Denmark, France, West Germany, Iceland, Luxembourg and Norway all allow access both to computerised and paper records. So too do bills or proposals in Greece, Japan, Spain and Switzerland. The British government, however, remains determined to restrict the UK Data Protection Bill to computerised records only – allowing no access to the vast number of records which in practice contain most of the information that the individual may need to see.

The measures now needed

Members of the public should have a statutory right of access to information held about themselves by public bodies. The broad principles of such a measure might be as follows:

1. Public agencies providing services or with the power to affect the right and liberties of the individual shall be required to publish a list of the types of records they hold on named individuals.

2. All individuals (or with their permission their parents or guardians or representatives) shall have a statutory right of access to those files or records.

3. The access should be prompt and a maximum period for response should be laid down.

4. Individuals should have the right to copy or obtain copies of material in their files.

5.   Individuals should have the right to request that inaccurate or misleading information be corrected. If the record-holding body does not agree, the individual should have the right to a formal hearing. If there is still no agreement, the individual should have the right to put a note on the record registering his or her disagreement. If appropriate there should also be the further right to appeal to the courts or an independent arbitrator.

6.   The record-holding body should publish a list of authorised bodies having access to information on the files, and should record on each individual's files the bodies to which access or information from the files has been given. The rights to challenge and correct information should also apply in these circumstances.

7.   The record-holding body should not be permitted to disclose the contents of personal files to other than the authorised bodies without the written permission of the subject of the file.

The main exemption to such procedures would be to protect private information about third parties that may also appear on the individual's file. This should not normally be disclosed to the subject of the file unless it directly affects them. Equally, the identity of a member of the public providing information about the subject of the file in confidence may need to be protected, although the information itself should be available to the individual. (An exemption of this kind is necessary to protect, for example, neighbours who may report cases of child battering and who believe they may themselves be exposed to risk of violence if their identity is revealed.) There may need to be further tightly drawn exemptions to cover other, similar situations, when disclosure would expose some individual to serious physical or other risk.

Such changes would inevitably have a major impact on the way records are kept. Most importantly, record-keepers would be inhibited from allowing subjective or pejorative remarks to find their way on to the record, even by accident. That will make records fairer – and probably improve their quality all round.

Most people will probably never want to see their records: it is likely that only when they believe they have been treated unfairly will they have any incentive to seek access to what has been written about them. If the record does contain damaging remarks, or inaccuracies, this will give them an essential opportunity to have these corrected and perhaps reverse unfavourable decisions that may have resulted from such information. If the record does not confirm their suspicions, then the fact that they will have been able to see it for themselves will do more than anything else to strengthen their confidence in their doctor, social worker, childrens' teacher or whoever else is recording information.

Most people who see their records will probably find that they are no more than a fair and straightforward account of what has taken place. The fact that the record-keeper will know that they may see what is written will itself help ensure that this is so.

PART 3
FREEDOM OF
INFORMATION

6 FoI IN OTHER COUNTRIES

JAMES MICHAEL

Freedom of information legislation is a global trend. Except for Sweden, whose Freedom of the Press Act has been part of the constitution since the early nineteenth century, all of the national laws opening up government records to the public have been passed in the last twenty years. Nearly all of those countries have also legislated on the related subject of data protection, frequently in the same legislation, or at least at the same time.

'Open government' is probably a more accurate description than freedom of information, because the purpose of all of these laws is to provide a legal right of the public to inspect government records. Such laws always involve issues of personal privacy, and this is why they overlap with data protection. If there is a general public right to see public files, there will usually be an exception to protect personal privacy.

Legal rights of access to government records have been introduced in most of the democracies mentioned in this chapter to make freedom of expression more than just a right to let off steam. In public debates on almost any issue the side which knows what it is talking about will usually win, and that knowledge is all too often locked in government filing cabinets. Establishing such legal rights has been seen as an extension of traditional freedom-of-speech values, providing a method by which democratic argument can be a matter of informed opinion.

Several issues have repeatedly arisen on the subject of open government legislation. The first is whether openness should be legally enforceable at all. Successive British governments have argued that it can be achieved without legislation, and that countries with such legislation are not noticeably more open than the United Kingdom. This argument is not particulary persuasive to journalists or researchers who have to travel to the United States to get information which is not available in Britain, but it survives in proposals for various codes of conduct rather than legal rights.

There will always be exceptions to any public right of access to government records, which raises difficult questions about what they should be and what form they should take – whether they should be narrow and specific or broad statements of reasons that justify secrecy (e.g. national security). This is closely related to another question, which is who is to decide whether particular records are exempt from disclosure. It is often said that this is the *only* issue, and that freedom of information laws simply transfer the power to disclose information from the elected government of the day to others such as judges or ombudsmen. But this argument ignores an essential element, that of self-interest: a Minister who wishes to remain in office and to see his policies carried out has powerful reasons for not disclosing information that will aid his critics. It is essential in any legislation that decisions in particular cases be made by someone who is as independent of the government as possible in order to avoid such self-interest. It is also important that such an independent arbiter be given clear rules about the reasons that will justify refusal of a request for access to records. With very few exceptions, the disclosure of government information is discretionary; the purpose of legislation is to make such decisions a matter of law, to be implemented by someone as free from self-interest against disclosure as possible.

Similar questions arise concerning data protection legislation. Should it be limited to personal information processed by computers or extended to manual records? Should it be limited to records maintained by government or include records in the private sector as well? A few countries include information on 'legal persons', such as companies, in their data protection laws.

All of these questions, and many others, have been considered in several countries in the past few years. Some of the answers reflect different methods of achieving the same purpose. Others represent refusals to accept the basic notion of open government, or half-hearted compromises. The countries which have legislated have usually considered the experience of those which have gone before. This the UK can usefully do.

Sweden

Sweden's law on public access to official documents is by far the oldest in the world. It was passed in 1766, and was restored in 1810 after a period of political turmoil. It is closely related, both in principle and historically, to the office of *ombudsman* (which has been successfully exported to a number of countries, including the UK).

The law is called the Freedom of the Press Act, although the right of access to public records is not limited to the press, and it is a part of the constitution. It is a legal right, rather than a mere statement of intention, and it is subject to exceptions. These exceptions exist at two levels. The first is in seven general principles which the Act says will justify secrecy; the second is in the extremely detailed provisions of the Secrecy Act of 1980.

The first of the seven principles justifies restrictions on disclosures *'considering the security of the Realm or its relations to a foreign state or to an international organisation'*, which is very similar to the first exemption to the US Freedom of Information Act for records 'properly classified' in the interests of defence or foreign relations. Another principle for restriction 'in the interest of prevention or prosecution of crime', is equivalent to a US exemption for 'investigatory records compiled for law enforcement purposes'. The Swedish principle for restrictions for *'the protection of the personal integrity or the economic conditions of individuals'* has a US counterpart in exempting records from disclosure if it would amount to a 'clearly unwarranted invasion of personal privacy'.

Apart from these there is no direct equivalence between the exemption principles of the Swedish Act and the exemptions of the US Act. However, there is a similarity between the Swedish definition of an 'official document' and the US exemption from disclosure for 'inter-agency or intra-agency memoranda'. Both deal with the subject of 'working papers' containing advice on policy decisions. The effect of both seems nearly the same, only achieved by different methods. The Swedish way is by a definition of an 'official document', which is more restrictive than the US definition of a 'record'. Both systems require the disclosure such advisory 'working papers' after the decisions based on them have been taken.

Swedish exemptions for commercial information are rather broader than those in the United States, taking together the principles concerning *'the central financial policy, the monetary policy, or the foreign exchange policy'*, *'activities of a public authority for the purpose of inspection, control, or other supervision'*, and the *'economic interests of the State or the communities'*. There is also a principle, apparently not much used, to restrict documents in *'the interest of preserving animal or plant species'*.

Complaints and appeals

The interpretation of these principles, and of the far more detailed provisions of the Secrecy Act, is done in two ways: by a legal appeal to an administrative court, with further right of appeal to the Supreme Administrative Court, or by complaint to the ombudsman (called the JO, from the official title, *justitieombudsman*). The ombudsman system is less formal. Although a decision by the JO that records should have been disclosed is not legally binding, it is usually persuasive. One provision, that an 'appeal against a decision by a member of the Government shall be lodged with the Government', is often misunderstood, especially by British readers who assume that Ministers thus have the final decision as to whether records must be made public. Most Swedish administration, however, is carried out by large agencies which are not under ministerial control. With the exception of the Foreign Ministry, Swedish ministries are small planning bodies which have no responsibility for administration.

Appeals seem to be about evenly divided between the JO and the administrative courts. An international survey by the British Civil Service Department in 1979 showed that in one year there were 100 complaints to the JO, and 50 to the Supreme Administrative Court, that did not include the many complaints made to the lower administrative courts.

Either public or secret
Strictly speaking, government documents in Sweden fall into one of two categories: either they are public documents which can be inspected by anyone as a matter of right, or they are exempt from such disclosure and must be kept secret. On the surface there seems to be little room for an intermediate category of documents which can be disclosed at the discretion of government or which can be 'leaked' by civil servants without being penalised, but in practice this is not the case. Many of the provisions in the Secrecy Act of 1980 justify a refusal to disclose documents if disclosure would harm a particular public or private interest, but although an authority may thus have a reason to justify a refusal to disclose, it will not necessarily require such a refusal. It is only in the case of documents containing information from a person or company that the government is clearly bound not to disclose without the consent of the originator. As for the leaking of documents, civil servants are protected from penalities more by the effects of various provisions than by any specific authority. If a leak is made to the press, it is very difficult for the person responsible to be punished unless espionage is involved. One provision of the Freedom of the Press Act says that only the registered editor of a journal is legally responsible for what is published. Another, called the anonymity principle, generally protects the identity of those who provide information to the press, although this apparently does not extend to handing over government documents.

Data protection
Sweden was the first country to enact a national data protection law. Although individuals already had general rights of access to records about themselves, it was felt that the automatic processing of personal information required additional legal safeguards. The Data Act of 1973 was concerned with information about natural persons that was handled automatically, in both the public and private sectors. It includes a basic right of subject access and a thorough system of administrative regulation by the Data Inspection Board. The Board has extensive authority to attach conditions to licences which data processors of personal data must have. The Board also administers two other statutes, the Credit Information and the Debt Recovery Acts, which are concerned with consumer credit information (roughly similar to the US Fair Credit Reporting Act of 1970 and the British Consumer Credit Act 1974).

Other Scandinavian countries
Norway and Denmark have also legislated on the related subjects of open government and data protection, although their open government statutes have been more recent and weaker than Sweden's. Norway only passed its open government law in 1970, after a series of commissions and political battles. The Administrative Procedure Act of 1967 already provided some access to official records for those affected by a particular administrative decision, much like a provision of the US Administrative Procedure Act of 1946.

The Norwegian public access law is subject to very general exemptions. The government can exempt whole classes of documents by decree, and agencies can refuse access to documents if they would give an 'obviously misleading picture'. A Ministry of Justice memorandum says that records can be refused to 'the mentally ill, inebriates, small children, rowdies, and slanderers'.

The Privacy (Personal Registers) Act became law in 1978. In some ways, Norway went further than most other countries with its data protection legislation: the law covers computerised information in both public and private sectors, and includes manual files held by government; it also includes both natural and legal persons. There is a near-absolute right of subject access, and an administrative Data Surveillance Service.

Denmark's Law on Publicity in Administration, which was passed in 1970, is much weaker than the Swedish counterpart. But it is relevant to countries with Westminster-style constitutions because Denmark does not follow the Swedish practice of separating ministries as small planning bodies from large semi-autonomous administrative bodies. As in Norway, the right of parties in administrative proceedings to see relevant documents came first, in the Law on Party Access in Administration of 1964.

As in Norway, the exemption from the general right of public access are very generally drawn, including one exemption to allow secrecy if it is 'required by the special character of the circumstances'. It also allows the government to make the final decisions about secrecy in designated areas. Enforcement of the law, however, is left almost entirely to the ombudsman.

Denmark also passed two related data protection laws in 1979, one for government and the other for non-government databanks. Both are supervised by a Data Surveillance Authority, and both apply only to computerised systems of pesonal information. Government databanks are regulated only if they contain information on natural persons, but commercial databanks are regulated if they contain information on natural persons or on 'institutions'. There is no general right of public access, although it may be required by the Data Surveillance Authority.

France

The French law on open government in 1978 came as something of a surprise. In a 1977 comparative study called *Government Secrecy in Democracies* France was classified along with the United Kingdom as a country in which the government's privilege to conceal was valued more than the public right to know. A committee on government information had been established in 1977, and it recommended in its 1978 report that there should be a general principle of public access to government records. The law was passed in July of 1978, and went into effect at the end of the year.

The law established the general right of public access, with an independent Commission to monitor the application of the law and to hear complaints from those denied access to documents. The exceptions are worded in fairly general terms, including the usual subjects of defence and foreign affairs, national finances, *sub judice* matters, subjects of personal privacy, commercial secret, and other legally protected secrets. The first exception is probably the broadest, exempting documents from disclosure if they concern 'secret discussions of government and other authorities concerned with the functions of the executive'. The law applies to both national and local government, and has a comparatively broad definition of what constitutes an official document. Like the US law, the exemptions may justify refusing access to a document if it is considered that disclosure would adversely affect one of the specified interests.

Enforcement resembles Swedish law in having two avenues of appeal: to the Commission and the administrative courts. But it differs from Sweden in making the Commission the first body to hear appeals. The Commission has forty members, with one member each from bodies such as the Senate, the National Assembly, local and regional government, the universities, the Council of State, and the Supreme Court of Appeal. There are only two government members.

Time limits on handling requests for documents are specific and strict, as under the US Act. Failure to reply within two months is deemed to be a refusal. The Commission must then make a recommendation to the government authority within one month, and the authority then has two months to accept or reject the recommendation. In 1979 and 1980 the Commission recommended disclosure in 175 cases, and recommended withholding in thirty-three. Of the disclosure recommendations, 75 per cent were accepted by the government authority.

France passed a data protection act in 1978, after considerable publicity and a commission report on the subject. The law covers both public and private sectors, includes both automated and manual files, and has a strong independent enforcement body. It originally was intended to include files on legal as well as natural persons, but was changed before it became law.

Netherlands

The Dutch open government law was also passed in 1978, but it appears to be far less effective than the French law. One interesting feature is that it establishes a right of access to 'information' instead of the more usual right to inspect and copy documents. The exemptions are in very general terms, excluding from disclosure opinions, 'incomplete data', commercial information and, along with the other usual exemptions, information that might 'endanger the unity of the Crown', as distinct from the security of the state.

The law does, however, provide for an independent review body in the Council of State, which serves both as the supreme administrative court and an advisory body on proposed legislation. Data protection legislation has taken longer in the Netherlands than in other countries, but at least an interim measure should soon come into force to enable ratification of the Council of Europe Convention on the subject.

Austria

Austria has had an open govenment law at the federal level since 1973, but it is so general that it amounts to little more than a statement of good intentions. It is in the form of an amendment to the Federal Ministries Act establishing a 'duty to inform'. But this is qualified heavily by the constitutional obligation of civil servants to keep information secret when it is in the 'interests of the administrative authority' or of parties concerned. Guidelines explaining the 'duty to inform' are fairly restrictive. Inquiries must be specific, and there is no duty to disclose information until after a tangible decision has been reached. Requests can be rejected if they would require evaluation or sifting of voluminous papers. Like the Dutch law, there is no duty to allow inspection of documents, but only to communicate their contents. But refusals to disclose information can be contested by appealing to the administrative courts.

In data protection, however, Austria has gone at least as far as most other European countries. The 1978 Data Protection Act proclaimed broad principles, established an elaborate enforcement system, and set up a timetable for bringing the law into effect. The law covers both government and private sector databanks, and protects information on both legal and natural persons. It is largely, but not entirely, concerned with automatically processed information. There is a basic right of subject access, including a right of correction. Enforcement is through both the ordinary courts and an administrative Data Protection Commission, subject to a supervisory Data Protection Council.

United States of America

The Freedom of Information Act was passed in 1966, and heavily amended in 1974 to strengthen the general right of public access to federal government records. It was preceded by a number of similar state laws, the first apparently being a Louisiana statute in 1912. Under the Administrative Procedure Act of 1946 there had been a right of access to federal records, but it was limited to records pertinent to an administrative claim.

The FoI Act requires some government records which establish administrative rules of practice to be published routinely. Other records are to be made available for inspection and copying on request, and can be withheld only if their disclosure would damage one of the interests described in any of the nine general exemptions. The only way in which disclosure can be enforced is by a successful appeal to the federal courts.

The nine exemptions

The first exemption is for *information which may be withheld in the interests of defence or foreign relations*. But in order to be kept secret the records must have been 'properly classified' in such interests, and the federal courts have the final decision as to whether classification was proper. This was established by the 1974 amendments to reverse the interpretation made by the Supreme Court in 1973 in a case brought by several members of Congress. The courts have the power to examine documents in private in determining whether the classification was justified.

The second exemption, for *internal personnel rules and practices*, has been fairly narrowly interpreted as applying only to minor 'housekeeping' matters. In particular, it does not exempt instruction that would affect a member of the public because, in the words of one Supreme Court justice, 'secret law is an abomination'.

The third exemption is for *information which has been exempted from disclosure by another statute*. An amendment in 1976 made it clear that other statutes will only justify secrecy if they leave no discretion as to secrecy or publicity. The fourth exemption is for what are usually described as *'trade secrets'*. It is the most frequently litigated of the exemptions, and the courts have worked out fairly clear tests as to when commercially confidential information can be withheld. It is not enough that the information has been given to a government agency with an 'in confidence' label. Refusal of disclosure on request is only justifiable if disclosure would cause substantial harm to the competitive position of the parties from whom the information had been obtained, or, if it was provided voluntarily, if disclosure would make it difficult for the government to obtain similar information in the future.

The fifth exemption is largely to *preserve confidential advice*. It does not include factual information such as statistics, and advice is only protected from disclosure until a decision based on it is taken. The sixth exemption protects *personal information from general release if it would amount to a 'clearly unwarranted invasion of personal privacy'*. It is clear now that this is not a reason for refusing to disclose information to the person concerned, although that was attempted in the early years of the law. It is the only exemption that requires a balancing test to determine whether the invasion of privacy by disclosure may be 'warranted' by the reasons for the request. An illustration of this was judicial refusal to order disclosure of names and addresses of people who had registered with tax authorities as home wine-makers when the purpose of the request was that a manufacturer wanted to send them advertisements.

The seventh exemption protects *'investigatory records compiled for law enforcement purposes'*. This was heavily amended in 1974. Records are now exempt if disclosure would cause any of six types of harm to law enforcement, including interference with active investigations, prejudicing a fair trial, unwarranted invasion of personal privacy, impairing confidential sources, disclosing investigative techniques or endangering the safety of law enforcement personnel.

The eighth exemption protects *records relating to banks and other financial institutions*, and there have been almost no cases under it. The ninth exemption protects information relating to *petroleum sources*, and it too has hardly been interpreted.

Privacy Act and other laws
The closest thing to a data protection law in the United States is the Privacy Act of 1974. This includes both manual and automated records on natural persons, but is limited to those maintained by the federal

government. Although it establishes some administrative rules, such as not using personal information for purposes other than those for which it was provided, there is almost none of the continuing administrative supervision that is characteristic of data protection legislation. Instead, the major method of enforcement is by the subject's right of access.

This overlaps with the right of subject access as part of the general rights under the Freedom of Information Act. The major difference between the two is that the Privacy Act provides a right of correction. On the other hand, the Privacy Act has two general exemptions that effectively protect all the records of the Central Intelligence Agency and many of the records of the Federal Bureau of Investigation. So requests for subject access to the CIA and FBI might be granted under the Freedom of Information Act, but without the right of correction under the Privacy Act.

Some other US statutes also provide rights of subject access. A law popularly known as the 'Buckley Amendment' gives parents and students the right to see student records held by educational institutions that receive federal funds. The Fair Credit Reporting Act is very like the British Consumer Credit Act in giving individuals the right to see and correct information held on them by credit reference agencies.

Other federal laws to encourage open government have also been passed recently. The Federal Advisory Committee Act was passed in 1972 to regulate the system of advisory meetings between regulatory agencies and the regulated industries. Consumer groups wanted such meetings to be held openly, and the act requires that notice be given, records kept, and members of the public be allowed to attend. The 'Government in the Sunshine' Act of 1977 establishes similar rules for meeting of boards at the heads of various federal agencies. These must generally be open to the public, and justifiable reasons for meeting in private are almost exactly the same as the reason to justify withholding documents under the Freedom of Information Act.

It is clear that the exemptions under the Freedom of Information Act are only reasons that will justify withholding records: they *allow* secrecy, but do not *require* it. So there is still a broad discretion on the part of government to disclose some records. There is also some statutory protection given to civil servants who leak information by the 'Whistleblowers' (Civil Service Reform) Act of 1978. This would not apply to leakers of information that was required to be kept secret by statute or in the interests of national defence or foreign affairs. But otherwise, the Act protects a civil servant who discloses information which he reasonably believes to show 'a violation of any law, rule, or regulation', or 'mismanagement, a gross waste of funds, an abuse of authority, or a substantial and specific danger to public health or safety'. Administrative sanctions are prohibited, and an Office of Special Counsel is established to enforce the Act.

Pros and cons

A composite criticism of the Freedom of Information Act frequently heard goes something like this: 'it is exorbitantly expensive, diverts government resources from governing to no discernible benefit, and is used almost entirely for industrial espionage and by criminals'. In fact, government agencies have routinely inflated the costs, sometimes allocating public relations expenses to the Freedom of Information Act. When the Privacy Act was passed the government estimated that it would cost ten times what the actual reported cost turned out to be. And the cost must be weighed against benefits, which are probably unquantifiable. It is difficult to calculate corruption that does not take place because of public scrutiny, or the cost to American society both in financial and human terms of dangerous drugs and contaminants that might have been approved if the records about them had not been made public. But these things should at least be borne in mind, along with the fact that government agencies do not object to the cost of 'public information' programmes about what they claim to be doing right.

As for the users, industrial espionage is a conclusion rather than an argument. Information provided by companies is not necessarily a legitimate trade secret just because the company wants it kept from the public. The most important 'trade secret' case concerned information provided by Chrysler Corporation to the Department of Defense, which was prepared to disclose it in response to a request from a pressure group. Chrysler sued to stop the disclosure in what is known as a 'reverse' FoIA suit. The Supreme Court decided that commercial confidentiality did not justify secrecy in these circumstances. The information concerned statistics on the employment of ethnic minorities.

Use of the Act by criminals is often alleged, but rarely proven. Even when requests were made by criminals there is no proof that the information was used for criminal purposes. The argument comes mostly from the FBI, which alleges that its sources of information 'dry up' out of fear of retaliation, although in fact there is a specific exemption for the identity of informants. The FBI arguments should be weighed against the fact that the FBI programme of illegal surveillance and harassment of political minorities came to light only after a successful Freedom of Information Act request.

Canada

During the 1970s both Canada and Australia were considering open government and privacy legislation, both at the national and provincial/state levels. New Zealand began serious consideration of the subject slightly later, but legislated at about the same time. All three countries are particularly relevant to the United Kingdom because their constitutions are based on the Westminster model, with New Zealand's being virtually identical; thus freedom of information legislation in all three countries now makes it difficult to argue convincingly that such laws are fundamentally incompatible with Westminster parliamentary government and ministerial responsibility.

Canada was not the first to legislate, by a few months, but its Act is almost certainly the most effective. It was influenced by the experience of the United States, and it began with privacy legislation similar to the US Privacy Act. Part IV of the Canadian Human Rights Act came into effect in 1978, establishing a general right of people to see files held on them by government departments. The exceptions were similar to those in the US Act, but there was no provision for appeals to the courts. A Privacy Commissioner was established to enforce disclosures instead, although ministers would have the final power to decide.

The provinces also began to act. Nova Scotia passed a Freedom of Information Act in 1977, followed by New Brunswick in 1978. Ontario established a Commission on Freedom of Information and Individual Privacy in 1977 to research the issue.

The national Act, passed in July 1982, was initially introduced by Conservatives and then taken up by Liberals after a change in government. It establishes a legal right of access to government records, subject to exemptions that mostly, but not entirely, resemble those of the US Act. Like the US and French laws, it has specific time limits for dealing with requests (although the US limits have been weakened by judicial interpretation). Access must be granted or refused within thirty days, with possible extensions.

The exemption for diplomatic records is nearly absolute, and applies not only to information obtained in confidence from foreign governments and international organisations, but also to similar information from provincial, municipal, or regional governmental bodies. There is also a broad exemption for confidential policy advice, even after the decision based on it has been taken.

Enforcement is largely through the newly created Information Commissioner, who has wide powers to investigate and recommend disclosure. There is a requirement that interested third parties such as those who provided the information must be given notice and an oppor-tunity to present their arguments against disclosure if they so choose. The Commissioner reports annually to Parliament, and can make special reports when warranted. But the Commissioner, like the counterpart Commission in France, can only recommend. If the recommendation is not accepted, a further appeal to the federal courts is not possible for all types of records.

Since the Canadian Act has only been in effect for a short while it is too soon to comment on how it is working in terms of recommendations for disclosure and the degree of their acceptance by government. Nevertheless, it is interesting that the volume of requests thus far has been much greater for access to personal files under the accompanying

Privacy Act (successor to Part IV of the Human Rights Act) than under
the Freedom of Information Act. The first court case under the
Canadian Act was decided in May 1984. It was what US lawyers would
call a 'reverse FoIA' action in which a company objected to disclosure of
information about itself by a government department on grounds of
commercial confidentiality. The Federal Court ruled in favour of
disclosure to a journalist, although the decision may be appealed.

Australia

The Australian Freedom of Information Act was the first national law
in the Commonwealth, but only just. It became law in March of 1982,
and went into effect in December of the same year. It establishes a
general legal right of access, but is subject to conclusive exemptions far
wider than those in the Canadian Act. Its enforcement system is similar
to that of Sweden in one way: the office of ombudsman is an alternative
to a judicial appeal, rather than a preliminary arbiter.

The exemptions include a schedule to the Act which places twenty-
two government agencies completely outside the Act, and another
nineteen outside the Act with respect to particular documents. For
documents that are within the Act there are extremely wide exemptions.
Appeals can be made to the Administrative Appeals Tribunal, but in
many of the most important areas, a ministerial certificate against
disclosure for certain reasons is binding on the Tribunal. These include
documents affecting national security, defence, international relations,
relations with the Australian states, Cabinet documents, and internal
working documents.

The Act was amended in the autumn of 1983 to make disclosure
requirements slightly more effective. The Administrative Appeals
Tribunal was given the power to examine documents, although the
Tribunal still can only recommend disclosure and cannot override a
ministerial certificate. The amendments also provide for phased
retrospection, somewhat like that in the Canadian Act, to allow access
to documents created before the Act came into effect.

New Zealand

Privacy law came first, with a 1976 Act establishing a Privacy
Commissioner for the Wanganui Computer Centre, which processes
nearly all government records. The next major step was the appointment
of the Danks Committee to consider public access to government
information generally. The Committee reported in 1981, and its recommendations were largely reflected in the Act of December 1982, which
came into effect in July 1983. The Act announces a public right of
access to government records, subject to exemptions, and provides an
Information Authority, Information Units in government departments,
and a right of appeal to the Ombudsman.

The difficulty is that the minister, or in some cases the Prime Minister, has an absolutely final veto over disclosure of records. When the bill was being considered in Parliament it was said by ministers that the use of the veto would be highly unusual, and that the Ombudsman's recommendations would be followed in most cases. The Act came into effect in July 1983, and five ministerial vetoes had been given by the end of September. Considering that the Act requires twenty-one days between the Ombudsman's recommendation and the minister's refusal, the first report on the Act must be that a final arbiter who is independent of the government of the day is absolutely essential to effective freedom of information legislation.

Conclusion

Despite differences in history and culture, all of the countries considered here have recognised three basic requirements for effective freedom of information legislation. The first is that there must be a right of access to government records, without any requirement that people must prove their 'need to know'. Second, the exemptions from this rule of disclosure must be drawn as specifically as possible, to prevent harm to identified interests such as national defence and personal privacy. Third, when access to records is refused, there must be a right of appeal to some authority – court, ombudsman, tribunal or some combination of these – which is independent of the government. If the government is its own judge in deciding that secrecy is justified by an exemption, the law becomes no more than a statement of good intentions.

While there are limitations in most legislation, all of these countries are moving in the right direction, and most of them acted in the 1970s. Like the United States, many of them are likely to look again at their laws after a few years and take steps to improve them. All of them have acted to protect two closely related rights: the citizen's right to privacy, especially against government, through data protection laws; and the citizen's right to know more about how he or she is governed. The United Kingdom is reluctantly moving towards a data protection law, and that only to avoid being frozen out of international markets. In freedom of information this country lags further behind the rest of the world with every year.

Appendix: The Council of Europe

(Source: Tom Riley, *Journal of Media Law and Practice*, Frank Cass, London 1982.)

In 1977, the Legal Affairs Committee of the Council of Europe was given a mandate to study the question of Freedom of Information and Privacy.

On 1 February 1979 the report of its subcommittee on Freedom of Information of the Legal Affairs Committee was brought before the Parliamentary Assembly for debate and was subsequently adopted unanimously. It was then referred to the Committee of Ministers (the senior body of the Council whose members consist of the Foreign Affairs Ministers of each country) for consideration.

The resolution recommended that each member country of the Council of Europe adopt Freedom of Information and Privacy laws if it had not already done so. It read as follows:

Recommends that the Committee of Ministers:

a.   invite the governments of member countries which have not yet done so to introduce a system of freedom of information, i.e. access to government files, comprising the right to seek and receive information from government agencies and departments, the right to inspect and correct personal files, the right to privacy and the right to rapid action before the courts in these matters;

b.   instruct the Committee of Experts in Administrative Law or any other expert committee to make a full study on the question of access to government files;

c.   implement its decision taken in 1976 to insert a provision on the right to seek information in the European Convention on Human Rights;

d.   study whether and to what extent documents relating to activities of intergovernmental co-operation within the Council of Europe may be made accessible to the public;

e.   publish periodically, in an easily accessible form, the texts of resolutions it adopts;

f.   give notice to the public, whenever possible and appropriate, of draft texts of conventions and resolutions pending finalisation and/or enactment by its appropriate organs.

The Committee of Ministers then circulated the resolution to member countries, who in turn responded to the practicability of adopting such measures according to their individual constitutions.

The report (Document 4195 of the Council of Europe) presented to the Parliamentary Assembly also contained an explanatory memorandum on the different rights and existing laws in the member countries. The memorandum pointed out the differences between the Finnish and Swedish approaches and the Danish and Norwegian approaches to access. The laws of the former two countries list exhaustively the types of documents which are to be kept secret or confidential, while the latter two acts state that the right of access to documents shall not include certain types of documents. This system does not necessarily mean that the documents are exempt, but rather that the matter is left to the discretion of the public servant, providing there is no other statute in Denmark or Norway which prohibits access. The report concludes, in contrasting the two approaches, that the Finnish and Swedish systems are more precise and transparent and therefore offer more safeguards for publicity.

The most interesting recommendation is the one suggesting that the law should offer a right of quick appeal to the courts. This reflects the influence of the American legislation rather than any current laws in the Scandinavian or European countries, where administrative procedures are more common.

The report recommends, along the lines of the American FOI Act, that there be exemptions. It concludes that in all states where information laws do exist there are the following broad categories of exceptions to what may be released. These are generally agreed upon by information advocates although there are disputes about documents dealing with state security, because of the broadness of the term 'state security' (or 'national security' in USA and Canada).

The exemptions, as summarised by the Council's report, are:

- national defence and state security;
- foreign relations and relations with international organisations;
- commercial, financial or fiscal secrets;
- court proceedings;
- prosecution and prevention of crimes;
- personal or medical files as well as other information that would constitute a breach of privacy, but citizens may, and they surely should, have the right to information that concerns them personally.

This latter exemption on medical files and the right to see information which concerns one personally has been the source of much controversy, especially regarding the argument of whether a person who is terminally ill should be allowed access to a personal file. There is broad disagreement on this issue.

The general conclusions of the Report state that a person has a basic right to know and that access to information kept by Government is an essential part of democracy and a right which must be enshrined by all countries. It reaffirms the right of a citizen to inform him/herself of what the government is doing and why. To this end, as much information as possible should be made available, with the exception of that information which must be withheld for the performance of good government.

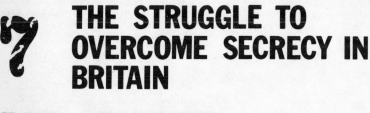

THE STRUGGLE TO OVERCOME SECRECY IN BRITAIN

DES WILSON

In Chapter 2 I observed that a reason for the high level of secrecy in Britain has been the lack of public demand for more information. Just as no-one questioned the remarkable powers of Section 2 of the Official Secrets Act when it passed the House in 1911, few (outside of Westminster and Fleet Street) have questioned them in later years. After all, the common assumption has been that the Act is about security secrets and spies, and thus its impact on everyday public life has not been widely understood by the ordinary citizen. The demand for freedom of information has only developed over the past twenty-five years, and this has reflected the increase in non-party political, voluntary activity and in pressure groups who have become experts on their subject and thus knowledgeable about what information is not available. Even so, those sufficiently motivated to work on the issue were few, and the same names have cropped up repeatedly – civil libertarian Tony Smythe, Professor of Politics James Cornford, consumer and environmental compaigners Charles Medawar and Maurice Frankel, former Ralph Nader aide James Michael, political lobbyist Martin Smith, local authority critic Ron Bailey, and journalist Peter Hennessy being some.

The Fulton Report

Ironically, it has been the occasional excesses of secrecy (excesses, that is, within a system that is already excessively secretive) that have sparked the main advances. The first notable blow to be struck, however, was from a more respectable quarter, with the publication in 1968 of the report of the Committee of the Civil Service led by Lord Fulton, the Vice-Chancellor of Sussex University. It argued that there was excessive secrecy and said:

> The increasingly wide range of problems handled by government, and their far-reaching effects upon the community as a whole, demand the widest possible consultation with its different parts and interests . . . It is healthy for a democracy increasingly to press to be consulted and informed. There are still too many occasions when information is unnecessarily withheld and consultation merely perfunctory . . . It is an abuse of consultation when it is turned into a belated attempt to prepare the ground for decisions that in reality have been taken already.

Harold Wilson's Labour administration published in June 1969 a White Paper based on what it claimed to have been an Inquiry (recommended by the Fulton Committee) 'on a wide inter-departmental basis'. As this had been an internal inquiry, and its deliberations had been confidential, there was some irony in this. In common with the views of all politicians when in power, it was less than enthusiastic about freedom of information. More 'information' was already being published, it said. In quantity this was probably the case, both because the state had encroached on more and more aspects of national life, and the bureaucracy increased accordingly, and because of the vast increase in departmental public relations men (sorry – 'information officers'). On the Official Secrets Act, it concluded that there was a case for protecting much official information from unauthorised disclosure and that a criminal sanction was needed for the protection of some of it. Then followed an argument which would be laughable if it were not seriously intended – that the Official Secrets Acts were no barrier to greater openness since they did not inhibit the 'authorised' release of information in any way. Clearly the authors of this White Paper either could not comprehend, or did not want to acknowledge, the concept of a public right of access, rather than an official right to disclose.

The Franks Committee
In 1971 came one of those excesses that has helped the anti-secrecy lobby. The journalist Jonathan Aitken, a critic of the British policy towards the civil war in Nigeria, had obtained and published in *The Sunday Telegraph* a confidential document on the Nigerian situation by the defence adviser at the British High Commission there. The newspaper, its editor, Jonathan Aitken and another journalist were prosecuted under Section 2 of the Official Secrets Act. They were all acquitted. Mr Justice Caulfield commented in his summing up that it was perhaps time the Act was 'pensioned off'.

It was widely assumed that the departmental committee on Section 2 of the Official Secrets Act 1911, chaired by Lord Franks, was set up by the Prime Minister of the time, Edward Heath, in response to that trial, but the committee were at pains in their report to stress that they had been appointed prior to the case. As I reported earlier, the Franks Committee found Section 2 'a mess'. It condemned its breadth and catch-all nature and complained that the drafting and interpretation of the Section were obscure: 'People are not sure what it means, or how it operates in practice, or what kinds of action involve real risk of prosecution under it.'

Section 2, it went on, had little to do with Section 1. 'It deals with information of all kinds, and it catches people who have no thought of harming their country. Many consider it wrong that such a provision should appear side by side with the rest of the Official Secrets Act.'

Franks reported that 'these factors convinced us that change was essential'. The only satisfactory treatment for a law suffering from so many defects was to sweep it away entirely. It concluded that a proper balance between openness and secrecy required a reformed law: 'Our major proposal is that Section 2 should be repealed and replaced by narrower and more specific provisions.' It proposed an Official Information Act making it an offence to disclose without authorisation a more narrowly defined range of information. Civil servants who leaked other information could not be prosecuted, but could still face disciplinary charges. The receipt of improperly disclosed information would no longer be an offence. The Franks Committee had, therefore, concentrated on closer definition of what should be secret, and how secrets should be protected – it did not extend its brief to look at the case for wider access to information.

In 1973 the Conservative Home Secretary at the time responded to Franks by stating that the Heath Administration accepted the essential recommendations of the Franks Committee but would want to consider further categories of protected information. This was to be the last official Conservative endorsement of either repeal of Section 2 or greater freedom of information. References to it were not to appear in subsequent manifestos, and with the advent of Mrs Thatcher to the Conservative leadership the trend, as we shall see later, was very much in the opposite direction.

Enter Labour

In 1974 a Labour Party sub-committee proposed a greater public right of access to official information and this led to a manifesto promise to this effect:

> We shall replace the Official Secrets Act by a measure to put the burden on the public authorities to justify withholding information.

After the return of a Labour government, the Queen's speech, in 1975, promised 'proposals to amend the Official Secrets Act and to liberalise the practices relating to official information'. The Home Secretary, Roy Jenkins, went to Washington to look at the Freedom of Information Act there. What happened is described in Kellner and Crowther-Hunt's *The Civil Servants*:

> Jenkins' visit to Washington . . . could scarcely have taken place at a worse time. The Freedom of Information Act had only recently been strengthened, over an attempted veto by President Ford, and against the wishes of the Justice Dept. Although it was too early to tell, a number of officials in the American Administration informed Jenkins and his colleagues that the newly-amended Act would be expensive to administer, and employ many extra civil servants. And because the new Act was so young, its supporters did not yet have evidence to counter the Justice Dept's assertions. Jenkins returned to London and announced his fears that a British freedom of information Act would be 'costly, cumbersome and legalistic'.

In 1976–7, after James Callaghan became Prime Minister, the issue developed momentum with the help of further governmental excesses. First, there was a massive inquiry into a leak to *New Society* magazine of a Cabinet discussion over child benefits. Then came 'the ABC Trial (so called because the three defendants were named Aubrey, Berry and Campbell). Two journalists and their informant – a former soldier – had been arrested after discussing intelligence monitoring of international radio communications by the then-secret Cheltenham GCHQ (not only is its existence now acknowledged, but it has, of course, in 1984 been the subject of a major political row over the Government's decision to deny union membership to those who work there). All appeared at the Old Bailey under Section 1 of the Official Secrets Act for offences relating to spying; these charges were later shown to be groundless and dropped during the trial. The former soldier was charged under Section 2 for unauthorised disclosure, and the two journalists with receipt of information improperly disclosed. The three were convicted but not punished under Section 2 charges. The main effect of the trial was to further discredit Section 2.

As a result of all this, Callaghan decided to act. He would replace Section 2 with legislation based on the Franks report to sharpen up the Act and make it more likely that when prosecutions were carried out they would succeed. There was no promise of freedom of information legislation of the kind referred to in Labour's election manifesto – Callaghan's plan was entirely defensive.

Nevertheless, Callaghan was surprised by the demands for freedom of information that arose at this time, not least from within his own party. Under pressure, he told the House of Commons: 'It will be our policy to publish as much as possible of the factual and analytical material which is used as the background to (major policy) studies. This will include material used in the programme analysis reviews unless – and I must make this condition – there is some good reason, of which I fear we must be the judge, to the contrary.'

That this was merely a gesture and that Callaghan completely failed to appreciate the full price we pay for secrecy is reflected in other remarks he made at that time: 'We shall look at every case to see whether we can make it available. The cost to public funds is a factor here, and we should like to keep that cost to a minimum. Therefore, arrangements will not be of a luxurious nature . . . .'

The Croham Directive

A few months later the famous Croham Directive (written by the then Sir Douglas Allen, Head of the Civil Service) was circulated. Ironically, this memo on greater freedom of information was itself confidential although it was leaked to the newspapers. Because of its importance to the debate, I shall quote from it at some length:

> During the debate on the address on 24 November last, the Prime Minister announced that it would be the government's policy in future to publish as much as possible of the factual and analytical material used as the background to major policy studies . . .

> The change may seem simply to be one of degree and of timing. But it is intended to mark a real change of policy, even if the initial step is modest. In the past it has normally been assumed that background material relating to policy studies and reports would *not* be published unless the responsible Minister or Ministers decided otherwise. Henceforth the working assumption should be that such material *will* be published unless they decide that it should *not* be. There is, of course, no intention to publish material which correctly bears a current security classification or privacy marking; at the same time, care should be taken to ensure that the publication of unclassified material is not frustrated by including it in documents that also contain classified material . . .

> The additional material will mainly consist of delivered presentations in the later stages of discussion and development of new policy. Some of these will probably, as now, take the form of Green Papers. Some may have kindred form, like the recent Orange Paper on transport. While most material will be released on the initiative of the dept., probably through HMSO, some of lesser importance, or of interest to a limited audience may well be put out through other means, such as publication in magazines, or in response to specific requests in the same way that a good deal of unpublished material is already made available to bona fide researchers. In some cases it may be preferable simply to publicise the existence of certain material which would be made available to anyone who asked. Consideration should also be given to the issue of bibliographies or digests so that interested parties are advised what material is available . . .

The normal aim will be to publicise as much as possible of the background material subject to Ministerial decision once they have seen the study and reached their conclusions upon it. When Ministers decide what announcement they wish to make, therefore, they will also wish to consider whether and in what form the factual and analytical material may be published . . .

There then follows a considerable section on how to do this as inexpensively as possible with remarks like 'Great care should be taken to keep costs to a minimum' etc. This is followed by an admission of the real motivation for the memorandum:

There are many who will have wanted the government to go much further (on the lines of the formidably burdensome Freedom of Information Act in the USA). Our prospects of being able to avoid such an expensive development here could well depend on whether we can show that the Prime Minister's statement had reality and results. So I ask all of you to keep this question of publicising material well on your check-list of action.

He then asked for a record to be kept of relevant items made available.

This was seen as a notable step, although careful reading, especially between the lines, showed that the effect would be minimal. The heavy emphasis on cost, and the automatic assumption on the basis of inadequate information that the USA Freedom of Information Act was 'formidably burdensome' and 'expensive', were in themselves a dampener. Nor was it in any event a major step towards freedom of information; the Official Secrets Act was still there, the 100-odd clauses of other legislation prohibiting disclosure were still there, and the stamps marked TOP SECRET, SECRET, CONFIDENTIAL, and RESTRICTED remained.

In 1978 a White Paper was produced in confirmation that Franks-type legislation was planned. It claimed that after the Croham Directive more official information was being published, although outside research did not substantially support this. On freedom of information legislation, the best it could do was promise an 'open mind'.

Freud's Bill

In 1978 the Liberal MP Clement Freud won the opportunity to introduce a Private Members Bill in the ballot, and decided to introduce freedom of information legislation. By that time, a number of anti-secrecy personalities had formed an organisation called the Outer Circle Policy Unit, headed by James Cornford, and they formed the main back-up team to Freud.

The Bill received a second reading on 19 January 1979. Freud began by reminding the House, and in particular Labour Ministers, that what he proposed was consistent with Labour's policies over many years – the Labour Party manifesto in 1979, the Queen's speech in 1975, the

Queen's speech in 1977, the Queen's speech in 1978, and so on – and then proceeded to make a mockery of the Official Secrets Act:

> If one wants to find out how to look after one's children in a nuclear emergency, one cannot, because it is an official secret; if one wants to know what noxious gases are being emitted from a factory chimney opposite one's house, one cannot because it is an official secret. A man who applies for a job as a gardener at Hampton Court was asked to sign form E74, in case he gave away information about watering begonias. What is worse, if someone is good enough to tell one, then one is an accessory to the crime. My contention is that Section 2 gives the Attorney-General more power than a bad man should have or a good man should need.

After a lengthy speech he concluded: 'A distinguished United States Senator said "A formidable check on official power has ever been what the British Crown feared and what the American founders decided to risk." My supporters and I invite Parliament to vote for that risk.'

The Home Secretary, Merlyn Rees, reminded the House that the Prime Minister had already said that they would not oppose the Bill: 'We believe in, and are committed to, greater openness in government.' He then went on to say, however, that he was not 'giving a blank cheque'; there were clearly reservations about what the Act would cover.

Labour's Green Paper

In March 1979, while support for the Freud Bill was gathering momentum, the Labour politicians in power, their manifesto promises a distant memory, produced a Green Paper as a defensive measure. It did its best to appear positive while arguing for voluntary disclosure rather than right-to-know legislation. It acknowledged that the 'catch-all effect of Section 2 is no longer right' and said that it was the intention that 'it should be replaced by provisions that would restrict criminal sanctions for unauthorised disclosure or communication to a strictly limited range of information'. It claimed an 'evolutionary approach' to freedom of information but 'nevertheless the government acknowledged that administration is still conducted in an atmosphere of secrecy which cannot always be justified'. It admitted that 'within parliament, it has become increasingly difficult for a Minister to be held to account for every single action of his department, and less practicable for parliament to scrutinise the increasing range of the government's work in the same amount of detail'. It further stated that:

> it is understandable that the individual should wish to satisfy himself as to the factual accuracy of information held on records such as those maintained by schools, hospitals and social services departments. The suspicion that public authorities (and some private bodies) hold information that could adversely

effect the interests of the individual, his family, his property, his neighbour-hood and indeed the total environment in which he lives and works, has led to the view that there should be a right of access to all such material, and this has come to be associated in the minds of many with the need for the right of access to information, held by public authorities, over much wider areas of administration.

It acknowledged that 'new measures are necessary to give further impetus to the process of making the government more open'. Nevertheless, in its conclusions, the lack of enthusiasm for radical action was clear:

> The government cannot accept that a statutory right of access which could affect adversely and fundamentally the accountability of Ministers to parliament is the right course to follow. There are other methods of securing more open government which do not carry such dangers . . . Resource constraints as well as experience overseas, suggests that a gradual approach is called for . . . A code of practice on access to official information, which the government was fully committed to observe would be a major step forward . . . Access would be given to official documents and information other than in fields that were specifically exempted from the operation of the code. The initiative in the release of material would no longer rest exclusively with the government. But accountability to parliament would be retained and the jurisdiction of the courts excluded.

Two months later the Freud Bill fell because the government fell and Mrs Thatcher was returned to power.

The Thatcher Government
In principle we should have been able to expect a positive approach to freedom of information. In her maiden speech in the House of Commons in 1959, Mrs Thatcher had introduced a Private Members Bill to create access for citizens to meetings of their local authority. 'The paramount function of this distinguished House is to safeguard civil liberties rather than to think that administrative convenience should take first place in law', she told the House in February 1960. From the start it was clear that what Mrs Thatcher felt to be appropriate at local level, was not appropriate at national level, at least not when *she* had power. By November 1979 *The Times* was making clear its displeasure in a leading article: 'She has passionately criticised the closed shop in many areas of British life. She should not now countenance a closed shop for information.

Her administration then announced a Protection of Information Bill. Section 2 of the Official Secrets Act would be replaced by measures to protect specified classes of information. There was, however, no public right of access. The classes of protected information proposed by Franks had been modified, and some dropped, but new ones covered the nationalised industries, telephone tapping and mail interception. The Bill was highly controversial. It created even more secrecy around the intelligence services, and this was to be its undoing, for had the Bill become law, Andrew Boyle would not have been able to publish his book *The Climate of Treason*, which led to the disclosure by Mrs Thatcher in the House of Commons that Anthony Blunt had been a Russian spy. The Bill was abandoned.

In 1981, Frank Hooley, a Labour MP, introduced a new Private Members Bill, based on the Outer Circle Policy Unit, but the government opposed it and it was defeated at its second reading. Peter Hennessy, the respected Whitehall reporter for *The Times*, wrote: 'In the immediate aftermath of the killing at the first opportunity last Friday afternoon of Mr Frank Hooley's freedom of information Bill by the government's payroll vote, it is difficult to see the Thatcher Cabinet is anything but totally dedicated to all that all-concealing administrative secrecy which has helped to produce an almost unbroken string of policy disasters for Britain since 1945.'

Proposals for reform

In January 1979 the Civil Service College had held a seminar on the question of more openness in government. Fascinating contributions were made by both Lord Croham and Lord Franks. Croham acknowledged the need for more open administration but advocated a cautious approach. Nevertheless, if the minute of the discussion is correct, he said that, 'In his view, the initiative in demanding official information should be given to people outside government, provided this right was limited in a satisfactory way.'

Lord Franks proposed a Select Committee on open government which would monitor the performance of government and exert pressure on it if necessary by claiming full debates in the House. Sir William Nield, a former Permanent Secretary in the Cabinet Office and at the Northern Ireland Office, wound up the event and, according to the minutes, suggested that 'there were a number of factors underlying the pressure for more openness in government'. These and the discussions that followed were recorded in the minutes:

1.   The public was regarded as having a right to full information, save where serious injury to the national interest would result.
2.   Traditional redress of grievances *now requires more openness*, over a wider field of government activity.
3.   The present legal position (Section 2 of the Official Secrets Act) *is untenable* and inconsistent with increasing openness of recent years.

In the following discussion those attending the seminar seemed to come down in favour of a published 'Code of Practice on Disclosure' which would be rather like the Highway Code: it would be non-statutory but have the approval of Parliament. This Code would deal with the disclosure of information by government, rather than by conferring rights of access on people outside government.

In its 1983 election manifesto Labour promised 'We shall introduce a freedom of information Bill providing a genuine system of open government and placing the onus on the authorities to justify withholding information.' In a reference to a Data Protection Bill, the same manifesto stated: 'We shall bring in data protection legislation to prevent the abuse of confidential information held on personal files and, subject to certain exemptions, allow individuals access to their personal records.'

A May 1983 Liberal policy document, reflected in their manifesto, said 'Excessive governmental secrecy which deprives the individual and his/her MP of necessary information to make mature democratic judgements should be broken down by repealing Section 2 of the Official Secrets Act and substituting an official information Bill on the lines of that introduced by Clement Freud in 1978.'

In August 1983 a joint Liberal/SDP Alliance Commission on constitutional reform proposed to:

(a)   create a public right of access to government and other official information;
(b)   create an individual right of access to information held by public authorities about that individual and protect the information against misuse;
(c)   protect official information to the extent necessary in the public interest to safeguard personal privacy;
(d)   establish procedures to achieve these purposes; and
(e)   reduce the unreasonably criminal broad sanctions of the Official Secrets Act, 1911, so that they apply only to the protection of compelling interests of the state and its agencies.

Authorities to be subject to freedom of information legislation would include central government departments, the Cabinet office, regional governments when established, local authorities, water authorities, and public utilities like British Gas.

In the autumn of 1983 the SDP made freedom of information its firm policy:

It is our view that reform of information law itself is now urgent, and that legislation to give effect to a coherent policy about information should rank high in the priorities of the next government. Such a policy should be based on one single principle: whoever needs information for any legitimate purpose within our society – including the accountability of power-holders to those over whom they exercise power – should be able to get it, unless there is some clear, specific and valid reason why it should be withheld from him.

The present party leaders

When the 1984 Campaign for Freedom of Information was launched in January 1984, it had the firm support of all three opposition leaders. Neil Kinnock of the Labour Party wrote: 'I welcome and support the 1984 Campaign for Freedom of Information . . . I want to emphasise both the importance of the issue itself and the commitment of the Labour Party to new Freedom of Information legislation which will strengthen Britain's democracy by requiring authorities to justify withholding information.'

David Steel of the Liberal Party wrote: 'Freedom of information is vital to the regeneration of our society . . . Our government is too centralised, too bureaucratic and too secretive, and is desperately in need of reform. The Campaign for Freedom of Information . . . has my best wishes for every success in its efforts.' David Owen for the SDP wrote:

> Since its inception the SDP has stood for more open government and the ending of an unduly secretive system of government. The public has a right to know whether it is being governed lawfully and efficiently. Whoever needs information for any legitimate purpose within our society should be able to get it unless there is some clear, specific and valid reason why it should be withheld. The SDP policy is to introduce a comprehensive Freedom of Information and Expression Act which would include such measures as the establishment of the principle that all government information is freely available unless otherwise decided. The legislation would also include the right of individuals to have access to information on themselves, subject to a Code of Practice defining exceptions and limitations. The law of privacy is in need of reform and all these issues have been the subject of detailed proposals for legislation by the Joint SDP/Liberal Alliance Commission on Constitutional Reform in their Report 'Towards a Constitutional Settlement'. I welcome the 1984 Campaign for Freedom of Information and pledge the full support of my party.

Mrs Thatcher, on the other hand, responded negatively. She wrote: 'I welcome any moves that will help to ensure that public demands for information are heard and as far as possible satisfied. But I firmly believe that major constitutional changes such as your campaign is proposing are inappropriate and unnecessary. We already have a clear policy to make more information available and the necessary machinery to do so.' It is already policy, she argued, to make available as much information as is possible and that 'the real question, therefore, is how the public interest in disclosure – or on the other hand, confidentiality – of particular information, is to be determined'. In the Prime Minister's view the answer lay in parliament:

> Under our constitution, Ministers are accountable to parliament for the work of their departments, and that includes the provision of information. A

statutory right of public access would remove this enormously important area of decision-making from Ministers and parliament and transfer ultimate decisions to the courts. No matter how carefully the rights were defined and circumscribed, that would be the essential constitutional result. The issues requiring interpretation would tend to be political rather than judicial, and the relationship between the judiciary and the legislature could be greatly damaged. But above all, Ministers' accountability to parliament would be reduced, and parliament itself diminished . . . In our view the right place for Ministers to answer for their decisions in the essentially 'political' area of information is in parliament.

On March 6 David Steel took the unprecedented step for a party leader of introducing his own Ten Minute Rule Bill to the House of Commons. He was assisted by the 1984 Campaign. Steel told the House: 'If ever there were a subject in which the collective will of parliament should prevail over that of the government of the day, surely this is it.'

All Members of Parliament were invited to put their names to the broad objectives of the 1984 campaign, and all eighteen Liberals and all four SDP members did so, as well as the Plaid Cymru and Scottish Nationalist MPs. Well over 100 Labour MPs immediately responded as well. The number of Conservatives, unfortunately, was in single figures. Thus while the 1984 Campaign and everybody concerned to achieve positive results on this issue, wished it to be an all-party issue, the Prime Minister had given her lead and the Party had largely followed.

Before I come to the 1984 Campaign itself, let's look now at what had been happening in the civil service over this period.

It is widely assumed that the civil service is the main opponent of freedom of information. It is not as simple as that. Closer examination of what the civil service unions have published on the matter, indicates that the problem is mainly at the top – resistance by a combination of Ministers and the most senior civil servants. In other words, the more the power, the more the desire for secrecy.

Two of the civil service unions, the Society of Civil and Public Servants, and the Institution of Professional Civil Servants, had actually called for repeal of Section 2 of the Official Secrets Act and for freedom of information legislation well before 1984.

Pressure from within the civil service

The **Institution of Professional Civil Servants** in 1979 passed a resolution stating that it recognised 'the need for a freedom of information Act which, while fully protecting national security and the individual's right to confidentiality, limits official secrets to a necessary minimum'.

In a subsequent paper on the subject, the Institute rejected voluntary action alone, saying 'it is now clear that such an approach needs to be supplemented by some form of freedom of public access to official information, backed by enforced provisions'. The reasons it gave were as follows:

1.   Although each political party has supported greater freedom of information while in opposition, they have been more reluctant to pursue it actively while in government. This reluctance is supported and enforced by many senior civil servants. The Information Directive of 1977 (The Croham Directive) has been increasingly ineffective as a means of securing greater openness. The increasing flow of information immediately following the Directive has recently dwindled to a trickle. It is unlikely, on the basis of past performance, that any measure to secure greater openness which leaves the initiative entirely with the policy-makers themselves whether Ministers or their officials, will break through the general preference for secrecy in decision-making.

2.   The 1979 Green Paper approach does not allow access to raw unpublished data processed by the government which, if available, would enforce the public not only to influence policy-making more effectively, but also enable them to make more informed choices in their personal lives.

3.   The Green Paper approach is more relevant to the policy-making functions than the executive functions of government. The latter often impinge closely on the daily lives of the public in two major respects. First there are the codes, guides and manuals governing the rights of individuals and organisations to state benefits and subsidies, obligations and penalties. These should be made available to the public with the deletion of those aspects which would be officially protected. Second, there is the growing concern of the public . . . about the information held by government and related agencies on private individuals and the growing practice of holding such information on computers which may be inter-departmentally linked. The public should know the type of information held by computer, they should be able to ensure that the information held is properly protected and used, and that it is accurate.

The paper then recommended that Section 2 of the Official Secrets Act should be repealed and replaced by a more precise definition of protected information. Moves towards more open government should be supported and encouraged. Support should be given to freedom of information legislation.

In 1978 the **Society of Civil and Public Servants**, representing executive grade civil and public servants, called for fundamental reform of the Official Secrets Act, for an additional review of the rules on disclosure, for a new Official Information Act to be based on the statutory right of access to, and use of, information except the defined restricted categories, for the use of criminal and administrative sanctions only for unauthorised disclosure of information in restricted categories, and for disclosure to the individual employee of information officially held about him or her. The Society stated that:

the simplest way of clarifying the position for all purposes – criminal and administrative – would be to lay down a statute with general right of access to official information which was not in an explicitly excluded category. Both seekers and possessors of official information could then operate on the clear criterion that, unless information fell into the restricted categories, it could and should be disclosed and used. The administrative rules could then be based on the simple position that civil servants could and should disclose information, unless it was within the restricted categories, thus mirroring the legislative position.

The Society said that the paying of public and political lip-service to open government, 'which in practice is mediated through administrative restraints', would lead to civil servants being blamed for unnecessary secrecy that should in reality be laid at the door of government policy.

Of even greater importance was the attitude of the **Association of First Division Civil Servants**. Late in 1983 it published a consultative document that conceded the need for greater freedom of information, but called for voluntary initiatives rather than legislation.

The First Division Association expressed concern about leaks but suggested that 'a reduction in secrecy would make it easier for government to keep confidential those matters which it considered most important to safeguard'. It said it 'seems pertinent to ask whether breaches of government confidences could be prevented by more positive means than plumbing. To some extent leaks have been prompted by a belief that government in the UK is excessively secretive by comparison with other democracies. This belief has some justification.'

Thus, it concluded, 'the government might like to consider whether some liberalisation of information might not be in its own interests'. It acknowledged that there was over-classification of documentation and that other material could be released earlier, and that often the consultations prior to policy-making were inadequate. It suggested an experiment in non-statutory freedom of information.

The First Division Association then accepted an invitation to meet the 1984 Campaign and talks began in March 1984. At the same time, a number of high-level former civil servants indicated some sympathy for anti-secrecy campaigners. Sir Patrick Nairne, appearing on the television programme *The Week in Politics* accepted the need to reform the Official Secrets Act and by no means ruled out freedom of information legislation. Sir John Hoskyns, former Head of the Number 10 Downing Street Policy Unit, in a public speech said: 'Open government . . . is not a fashionable option, but a pre-condition for any serious attempt to solve Britain's underlying problems.' He went on, 'With confidence and competence so much lower than they should be, it is not surprising that Whitehall fiercely defends its tradition of secrecy. The Official Secrets Act and the Thirty Year Rule, by hiding peacetime fiascos as though they were military disasters, protect Ministers and officials from embarrassment.'

The most notable contribution, however, came from one of Britain's most respected former civil servants, Sir Douglas Wass, Permanent Secretary to the Treasury in 1974–83, and Joint Head of the Home Civil Service from 1981–83, during a series of Reith lectures on BBC Radio 4. He said that the challenge facing any democratic society was to secure a more informed public: 'There is a need for governments on a systematic basis to publish the information they possess which will contribute to public understanding of policy issues.' He went on:

Having lived with (the) dilemmas for a very long time, I have become profoundly sceptical about the arguments for secrecy. Step by step over the years we have published more and more material which previous generations of officials had thought to be dangerous. In the event publication has caused very little, if indeed any damage. The onus, I now believe, ought to lie heavily on those who oppose publication to justify their opposition.

Sir Douglas made clear his opposition to unauthorised leaks, and also defended the need for some privacy in governmental decision-taking. He continued:

It is in the field of factual and analytical material that governments could and should play a more constructive part, for it is here that they process a wealth of data, much of which is not released to the private citizen or to parliament. Government departments commission research, carry out surveys, study what is happening in other countries and generally establish a good and thorough informational base upon which to make policy. They also, of course, have a substantial body of incidental evidence from on-going administration . . . most of this information would not be readily available to the public unless the government supplied it. Much of it is of some public interest and it is difficult to see why in a democracy it should not be published.

Claiming that there has been some action to increase freedom of information, Sir Douglas said that:

nevertheless a suspicion exists that departments do not go out of their way to disclose information – certainly information which sits uneasily with the chosen policy. It is unsatisfactory for parliament to have to rely on its own alertness and astuteness in eliciting material from the government. This state of affairs has aroused interest in some statutory obligations on the government to publish its privileged information or to provide access to its own records.

Sir Douglas provided support for those who say that in the absence of some controls a system of voluntary release of information would 'allow back-sliding'. He said 'this concern is entirely justified'. He stated that the reasons for deciding against publication have often been 'nothing more weighty than political embarrassment'.

Even on defence issues, government ought to strike a reasonable balance between openness and security. It was, however, outside the area of national security 'that I see little cause to be restrictive about publication'.

Looking at ways of improving the flow of information, he said that an information audit merited serious study. He considered the possibility of legislation and stated that in other countries legislation had 'allayed the anxieties of those who fear the damaging effecs of too much exposure. And it seems not to have led to any significant impairment of the efficiency of governments'.

1984 – fact or fiction?

In January 1984, the Prime Minister welcomed the New Year with a message to the public. Orwell's *1984* had been disproved, she said. Under her, freedom and liberty thrived. Almost immediately her Administration launched the first prosecution under Section 2 of the Official Secrets Act, having forced *The Guardian* in the courts to disclose the source of a leak. Next, seven police arrived with a search warrant under the Official Secrets Act at the offices of the environmental pressure group Friends of the Earth seeking the source of another leak. The following day the journalist Duncan Campbell, one of the defendants in the ABC trial, fell off his bicycle and was taken to hospital. The police took his bicycle away, read the documents contained in Campbell's bag, and as a result arrived at his flat the following day to search it for over seven hours. Once more they had a search warrant under the Official Secrets Act.

In the same week, I, as Chairman of the 1984 Campaign, received an extraordinary letter from the Minister for the Civil Service, Lord Gowrie. When the 1984 Campaign had been launched I had written, as a matter of courtesy, to the Permanent Secretaries as follows:

Dear Permanent Secretary,

I enclose the material published at the launch of the 1984 Campaign for Freedom of Information.

Additional copies can be purchased for circulation to colleagues.

We are anxious to have a constructive and friendly dialogue with Whitehall on this matter and would welcome your views.

Yours sincerely
Des Wilson

The following correspondence then took place:

Dear Mr Wilson   2 February 1984

I understand that you have written to the Permanent Secretaries of a number
of Government Departments, suggesing a 'friendly and constructive dialogue'
with your Committee about the material which you enclosed with your letter.

The Government's view has been made clear, and was set out in the Prime
Minister's letter to you of 9 December. Other political parties, as you yourself
have emphasised, take a different view. I am sure you will understand,
therefore, that given these political differences, the principle of Civil Service
impartiality should be preserved. This would make it altogether inappropriate
for Permanent Secretaries or other Departmental civil servants to take part in
the kind of discussion which you have in mind.

Yours sincerely
Lord Gowrie

Dear Lord Gowrie   7 February 1984

I have to say that I find your letter of 2 February astonishing.

First, my letter to Permanent Secretaries and the enclosed material about our
campaign was clearly an act of courtesy on behalf of our campaign, and I have
no doubt was understood to be so by the majority of them, and your response
is, therefore, at best heavy-handed and borders on paranoia.

That said, we do of course have arrangements in hand to meet Civil Service
unions, and I have no doubt they would take the same dim view as our
campaign of your attempt to stop reasonable dialogue between civil servants
and well-established public organisations on the way our governmental system
operates and how it can be improved.

I know this is 1984, but your position that once the Prime Minister and
colleagues have made up their minds, a subject no longer exists for discussion,
is Orwellian in the extreme.

It will be noted by all objective observers that a government that puts so
much stress on the rights of the citizen, individual freedom and democracy, is
literally terrified of discussion on how the rights of the citizens can be better
protected and our democracy made more healthy.

Yours faithfully
Des Wilson

Dear Mr Wilson   22 February 1984

I have to say that I find your letter of 7 February no less astonishing than you
found mine. I don't think you have understood what I wrote.

The Government does not have any intention of trying to inhibit general
public discussion of the objectives of your campaign or to suggest that 'a
subject no longer exists for discussion' just because we have a particular view
about it, and it is absurd on your part to suggest that it has. My letter was
concerned with something quite different – discussion with serving civil
servants who are advisers to Ministers. The rule is that civil servants should
not take part in public discussion of any matter of current or potential political

controversy. That is not a new rule: successive Governments have adopted it, and the principle is of very long standing. Its purpose is to maintain the political impartiality of the Civil Service. If civil servants are to serve impartially Ministers of any political party, they cannot expect or be expected to engage in public discussions on matters which, like your campaign, involve party political controversy.

Yours sincerely
Lord Gowrie

Dear Lord Gowrie   24 February 1984

Thank you for your letter of February 22.

You appear to miss the two fundamental issues at stake:

First, we are still a democracy, not a dictatorship. The election of an Administration of any political party makes that Administration the temporary custodians of our affairs, not the permanent controllers. Continual debate should take place involving all sections of the community about all aspects of national life. It has been made clear to me that there has been widespread dismay at every level of public life at the way the Prime Minister and yourself have in such a heavy-handed and obstinate way tried to destroy any debate on the issue of freedom of information before it has even begun. Fortunately, such an objective is beyond even your powers to achieve. In our initial approach to the Prime Minister, we sought only dialogue, and it is deeply regrettable that her response was to display a completely closed mind and to attempt to forcibly close those of her colleagues and senior civil servants.

Second, the issue at stake is not just one of broad political policy, but about the administrative workings of Whitehall and other statutory bodies. An open-minded Administration should always be prepared to encourage its servants to participate at least to some extent in dialogue on such matters, if only to put their expertise about how Whitehall works, and their reservations about the advantages or disadvantages of any proposed measures, on the table for the benefit of all concerned parties. In the case of freedom of information, a coalition of twenty-five respected national organisations with a considerable combined record of public service, some of them partly funded by government, sought a friendly and constructive dialogue with civil servants on a matter that directly affects them in their work. Had you written to say that you would like to feel that there were some boundaries to the involvement of civil servants in the debate, this could possibly have made some sense (at least in the context of the way your particular Administration works), but a refusal to allow them to discuss the matter at all is simply unacceptable.

Yours faithfully
Des Wilson

What had happened was that the Thatcher administration, reflecting the authoritarian, mother-knows-best attitude of the Prime Minister herself, had done more in a few weeks to underline the central message of Orwell's *1984* than the activities of all the anti-secrecy campaigners combined. She had provided firm evidence of the powers the state had under the Official Secrets Act, and further politicised the issue.

It was clear that her over-reaction was worrying the media, and also civil servants, who were annoyed by the Gowrie correspondence. One wrote to me about a civil service college course: 'Lord Gowrie was given a really rough ride by the civil servants on the course, who badgered him about the Croham Directive, Select Committees, 1984 Campaign and his draft letter to Permanent Secretaries about it, and foreign comparisons. For twenty minutes every question asked was about official secrecy.' But, to up-date the story of attempts to achieve freedom of information legislation in Britain, I must now introduce the 1984 Campaign itself.

The Campaign

My personal concern about the issue was long-standing but was intensified because I had since 1981 worked on the CLEAR campaign for lead-free petrol and been heavily involved with Friends of the Earth. As must be only too evident from Maurice Frankel's chapter on environmental secrecy, the frustrations I and my friends experienced because of the secrecy of both Whitehall and industry were immense. In particular, I was angered by my experience with lead in petrol.

In March 1981 the then Secretary of State at the DoE, Tom King, announced the decision not to move to lead-free petrol, but rather to reduce the level to 0.15 grams per litre by 1985. The CLEAR campaign was launched in January 1982 to seek to have that decision reversed. The immediate response by Ministers, notably the disastrous pair, Giles Shaw and Kenneth Clarke, was that our campaign was 'emotive', that our case that there was a health hazard was 'exaggeration' and that there was no evidence to bear out our fears.

Unbeknown to CLEAR, or the public, or MPs, or almost anyone else, as far back as March 1981, the nation's Chief Medical Officer of Health, Sir Henry Yellowlees, had circulated a letter to a number of Permanent Secretaries in Whitehall warning them that there was a health hazard, that 'hundreds of thousands of children are being affected'. He recommended decisive action.

Under the kind of freedom of information legislation we now propose, the advice of the Chief Medical Officer of Health would be available to the public. He is, after all, not a policy-maker, nor a politician, but a hired expert – in this case, an expert hired by the public, and there is no reason why his expertise should not be broadly available. However, in Thatcher's Britain, his warning, that hundreds of thousands of children are affected, is secret.

Fortunately, a Whitehall mole leaked the letter and CLEAR was able to publish it in March 1982. From that moment on, there was no way that ministers could sustain their defence of their positions, and no way they could any longer condemn CLEAR for its 'emotive' comments about the health risk, for Sir Henry Yellowlees' comments were as powerfully worded as our own. Nevertheless the secrecy over the advice of the Chief Medical Officer of Health had been maintained for over a year, allowed an incorrect decision to be made, and postponed the introduction of lead-free petrol by a further period. (Ministers had to capitulate to our campaign by April 1983, when it was announced that Britain would move to lead-free petrol by the end of the decade.)

This was only part of the secrecy. When the Royal Commission on Environmental Pollution decided to look into the lead question, the industries as well as campaigns like CLEAR, and ministries, submitted evidence. CLEAR circulated its evidence widely, sent it to the industries, and released it to the media. The UK Petroleum Industry Association, however, refused to share its evidence with CLEAR. It was typical. These industries feel answerable to nobody. When asked to provide the economic background to their claims that lead-free petrol would cost anywhere between 3p and 15p a gallon extra, the industries refused.

Once a decision was taken, and Giles Shaw had been moved from the DoE, I met with William Waldegrave, the newly appointed Minister with responsibility for lead pollution. I pointed out to him that the CLEAR campaign had been vindicated, whereas industry's many claims had been disproved by the Royal Commission on Environmental Pollution, as well as other reports.

In view of this, I put it to him that there should be an open debate about the economic and technical implications of the governmental decision. Industry should not be able to propose what it would cost to move to lead-free petrol, and to influence the choice of a date for implementation, without discussion with consumer and environmental bodies as well. Waldegrave said he took my point, but said that it would be difficult to publish all the information the industries provided. If they knew this was the case, they simply would not be forthcoming. Nevertheless, he promised by the autumn that he would publish a full outline of the technical and economic position, so that there could be wide-ranging debate. I confirmed his promise in a letter to him, and he did not contradict it.

Talks with the industries then proceeded in secret. Virtually on Christmas Eve – the last parliamentary day before Christmas – Waldegrave provided a bland reply to a planted question in order that he could pretend he had fulfilled his promise. The reply speaks for itself:

Over the last six months we have had formal discussions with the United Kingdom Petroleum Industry Association, the Society of Motor Manufacturers and Traders and other bodies about the introduction of unleaded petrol. There has also been a good deal of informal contact . . . Because *such negotiations are always delicate*, and because the *information we already have is in any case subject to revision, I do not want to go into particulars at this stage* [emphasis added]. I will report further when there is substantive progress to announce. In the meantime I am very grateful to the two industries for the help they have already given us.

Thus, despite the fact that the industry had been discredited in its technical and economic claims by objective judges, and despite the fact that the CLEAR campaign had been fully vindicated, together with the pressure from other consumer and environmental organisations, the same people – civil servants and industrialists – were once more meeting behind the same closed doors to work out their position together.

It was because of my experiences on these environmental issues that, in my capacity as Chairman of Friends of the Earth, I invited a number of voluntary organisations and pressure groups to a meeting in June 1983 to ask whether they, too, were frustrated by secrecy. I found widespread support for my proposal of a coalition to form a major campaign in the appropriate year of 1984. We decided to call it the Campaign for Freedom of Information, and – fortunately – all of the most experienced anti-secrecy campaigners to date – James Cornford, James Michael, Charles Medawar, Tony Smythe, Martin Smith, former MP Chris Price, Ron Bailey, and others – offered to participate. After much debate over our objectives (see next chapter), we set about the recruitment of support for the coalition. On 5 January, when the Campaign was launched, we were able to announce the support of twenty-five national organisations, over 150 Members of Parliament, over fifty Members of the House of Lords, and all three major opposition leaders.

Within weeks, a considerable number of other organisations had indicated they also wished to participate (by the Spring there were fifty in the coalition) and enthusiastic, well-attended launch meetings were held in a number of major provincial cities.

At the time of writing, March 1984, the campaign is well under way. It has already published two major 'secrets files', those on environmental pollution and access to individual files, which are largely covered in Maurice Frankel's chapters in this book. It has also been well received by the media. *The Guardian* stated:

It is a more than worthy cause: the campaign is being organised with considerable intelligence and impressive support; and perhaps most significant of all, there is already a perceptible nervousness in Whitehall about its chances of success. . . . It is not simply that the Official Secrets Act needs to be drastically revised and narrowed down. It is that the whole of British public life is pervaded by systematic secrecy and obsessive belief that the public should only be informed in exceptional circumstances. Democracy cannot flourish in such a climate, which can only change if the presumption changes in favour of the public's right to know.

The Scotsman described the Prime Minister's view that availability of information would 'undermine Ministers, and, ultimately, parliament' as 'a well-rehearsed piece of banal nonsense'; while *The Times* charged that the openness of administrations overseas, particularly those with Westminster-Whitehall style administrations 'ruins the traditional alibi of British Prime Ministers – which was wheeled out on cue by Mrs Thatcher yesterday – that such arrangements may be alright for foreigners, but they sit ill in the British system with its convention of Ministerial accountability to parliament.'

The Times further urged the Treasury and Civil Service Committee to look into the issue: 'It is too important to be entrusted to the hands of Whitehall and its penumbra of pressure groups. It is time for parliament to step in and shed light where there is heat.'

The Sheffield Morning Telegraph commented 'It is doubtful if any Prime Minister of any party would ever support such a Bill, whatever they may say in opposition. They have too much to lose. But that is probably the Bill's supreme justification.' *The Newcastle Journal* also spoke in favour of legislation:

> For our part, we have always believed the public interest can best be served by the disclosure of official information – except in cases where it might reasonably be deemed to be a threat to national security . . . The only way to force a reluctant officialdom to abandon current practices of concealment is through appropriate legislation which would give new rights to the individual. Official secrecy – especially to the degree that pertains in Britain today – conspires against the fundamental nature of democracy and distances the people from government at all levels and also from powerful vested interests.

Particularly encouraging was the response by local authorities to the investigation carried out by Ron Bailey and the Community Rights Project into the implementation of existing freedom of information laws and regulations. While some took exception to the criticism, others responded positively. Local media supported the campaign. For instance, the *Coventry Evening Telegraph* in a leading article stated:

> Failure by Town Hall staff to give information which should be available by law may arise from ignorance rather than a wish to be obstructive. But it is important that senior officers react constructively to criticism from the Campaign for Freedom of Information, for it is clear that there is a lot of re-educating to be done . . . The survey has shown dramatically how far councils are failing in their legal obligations. It is now up to councillors and chief executives to put it right.

On 6 February *The Times* revealed that the Cabinet Office had refused to release the results of its unannounced study of how effective the Thatcher administration had been in making information available to Parliament and the public. Peter Hennessy reported in *The Times* that the correspondence between Permanent Secretaries and the Cabinet Office which formed the basis of the study would, in the words of Lord Gowrie, Minister of State for the Civil Service, 'obviously not lend itself to publication'. As a result the correspondence would not be declassified until 1 January 2014.

From then on the successes came thick and fast: the coalition built steadily until the number of major organisations exceeded 50. In a spectacular week in May all of the civil service unions came fully on board, one after the other. These included the Civil and Public Services Association, the Society of Civil and Public Servants and the Institution of Professional Civil Servants, all of which passed resolutions in support of the Campaign. The major surprise however was the First Division Association of Civil Servants, which made headlines by supporting the principle of freedom of information and then deciding for the first time in its history to affiliate with a pressure group – The Campaign for Freedom of Information.

Sir Douglas Wass considered further his position, and announced that he was prepared to assist the Campaign. 'I now believe the case is made for repeal of Section 2 of the Official Secrets Act and legislation to give greater public access to official information', he said. Neil Kinnock wrote an article for Secrets newspaper stating his regret 'that the last Labour government succumbed to the temptation, left the Official Secrets Act unreformed, a Freedom of Information Act unlegislated'. He went on, 'I have already made plain my own commitment, and that of the Labour Party, to the introduction of a Freedom of Information Act. It is a commitment which will be honoured as a priority by the next Labour government.'

The Royal Commission of Environmental Pollution produced its tenth report with a heavy emphasis on the right to know. 'We see no case for withholding from the public information which regulatory authorities are entitled by statute to receive or obtain', it said. It recommended 'that a guiding principle behind all legislative and administrative controls relating to environmental pollution should be a presumption in favour of unrestricted access by the public to information which the pollution control authorities obtain or receive by virtue of their statutory powers, with provision for secrecy only in those circumstances where a genuine case for it can be substantiated.'

The Sarah Tisdall Case

In March 1984 the ability of the State to use Section 2 of the Official Secrets Act to strike fear into the hearts of potential leakers within the civil service was underlined by the Sarah Tisdall affair.

Miss Tisdall had worked in the private office of Sir Geoffrey Howe and obtained a memorandum written by the Secretary of State for Defence, Michael Heseltine, on how he would handle the public relations aspects of the arrival of cruise missiles in Britain. She photocopied it and delivered it in a brown envelope to *The Guardian* newspaper, which duly published it.

The government took *The Guardian* to court to force it to hand over the photocopies in order that the whistle-blower could be detected. *The Guardian* assumed that its position was protected under legislation entitling it to keep confidential the sources of its information, but the court ruled that it must hand over the documents. Shortly afterwards, Sarah Tisdall, a 23-year-old Foreign Office clerk, admitted that she was the leaker.

She was subsequently sentenced to six months in Holloway by Mr Justice Cantley who stated 'It must be made perfectly clear by example that any person entrusted with any material classified as secret, and who presumes to give themselves permission to publish it shall not escape custodial sentence'.

The sentence caused uproar. It was pointed out that at both *The Guardian* hearing and at Miss Tisdall's trial, the prosecution had emphasised that national security had not been endangered. Comparisons were made between Miss Tisdall's relatively trivial offence and that of the late Sir Anthony Blunt, who had been a major spy, but avoided prosecution.

The 1984 Campaign made a number of points about the Tisdall case:

First, we pointed out that Miss Tisdall had been imprisoned under discredited legislation. The use of an Act condemned by a Committee which had been specifically set up to look into it (the Franks Committee) and by politicians of all parties, including the present Home Secretary, was unacceptable.

Second, we pointed out that Miss Tisdall had no right of defence on the grounds that she had acted in the public interest. We were not saying, of course, that she would have been able to make such a defence, in this particular case, but we argued that she should at least have the right, as she would have done in the United States.

Third, we stressed our view that it was wrong that any unauthorised disclosure, except that which endangered national security, should involve a criminal prosecution and prison sentence. Internal disciplinary proceedings, and probable dismissal, would have been more than adequate.

The controversy raged for days, with only *The Times* and *The Daily Telegraph* defending the prosecution, and even those newspapers admitting that the sentence had been exceptionally severe.

While it would have been of little consolation to Miss Tisdall in her Holloway cell, the case did much to intensify criticism of excessive secrecy and the particularly secretive approach of the government of the day.

8 FREEDOM OF INFORMATION BY LAW: AN ALTERNATIVE TO SECRECY

DES WILSON

To begin contrarily, let me acknowledge that there is a need for some secrecy. Perhaps confidentiality is a more satisfactory word. The need falls under three main headings:

1. To protect the privacy of the individual.
2. To protect the community and the state, and other forms of organisation, from those who would for malevolent reasons use some kinds of information to cause harm. In the case of the state, protection may be necessary from foreign enemies; in the case of businesses, from competitors.
3. To enable frank and free opinion-sharing. Confidentiality is particularly justifiable in circumstances where exploratory exchanges of opinion take place and where it encourages greater honesty and flexibility.

Because it is necessary that any Freedom of Information legislation acknowledges these realities, I shall explore them first.

Necessary exemptions

Whenever there are proposals to reduce secrecy, the words 'national security' are bandied about. No-one would deny that there are some countries who are a potential threat to our own, and that some defences are necessary. It is only realistic to acknowledge that some confidentiality is necessary to preserve those defences. There is, of course, a need for careful debate on what does and does not affect national security, for overall defence policy and defence expenditure will remain matters for public and political discussion. Therefore it is necessary to define as tightly as possible what a replacement Official Secrets Act is intended to protect and what it is not. The introduction of FoI legislation in other countries has not adversely affected national security.

There are, of course, other kinds of information that need to be protected to safeguard the state and the community. The most carefully devised FoI Bill so far introduced to the House of Commons, written by James Cornford and colleagues and introduced by Frank Hooley, spelt out the necessary exemptions:

1. (1) Any document containing information the disclosure of which would or might impair:

    (a)   the defence or security of the United Kingdom, or any territory for which Her Majesty's Government of the United Kingdom has responsibility; or

    (b)   the relations or dealings between the Government of the United Kingdom and any other government or any international organisation of states or governments in the conduct of foreign affairs,

or would divulge any confidence of the Government of another country.

(2) Any document containing information relating to current proposals, negotiations, or decisions connected with alterations in the value of sterling, or relating to the reserves, including their extent or any movement in or threat to them.

(3) A document shall not be regarded as falling within 1(b) above by reason only that it concerns the relations between the United Kingdom and the European Communities or any acts or proceedings taking place within the organs of the European Communities (other than the European Council) or relating to Community affairs, except where such activities relate to the international relations of the European Communities themselves.

2. Any document relating to law enforcement or the investigation of crime, where disclosure would or might endanger the life or safety of any person, or be helpful in the commission of offences or in aiding escapes from any prison, or be likely to impede the prevention or detection of offences or the apprehension or prosecution of offenders.

3. Any document which would be privileged in legal proceedings on the ground of professional privilege.

4. Any document containing confidential information whose disclosure would cause substantial harm to the competitive positions of the parties from whom it was obtained or impair the ability of departments or authorities to obtain such information in the future.

While at the time of writing, the 1984 Campaign is considering the details of its legislation, it can be expected to contain exemptions broadly reflecting those in the Hooley Bill.

More contentious areas

A particularly tricky area is that of commercial confidentiality. Companies need to maintain some secrecy in competitive markets if they are not to be put at a considerable disadvantage; if a company has invested a substantial sum of money in the manufacture of a product that is better than those of its competitors, then it would be damaging to that company if the formula or technical details were readily available to others. On the other hand, as Maurice Frankel makes clear in Chapter 3 on environmental pollution, the secrecy of companies extends far beyond the need to protect themselves from competitors, and the legislation may need to be specific in defining what is genuine commercial confidentiality.

Other countries have also had no difficulty in providing protection for the individual within their FoI legislation – and rightly so. While the 1984 Campaign accords high priority to our right of access to our own files, it equally understands and supports the National Council for Civil Liberties and others who wish to reduce the right of access to those files by other people and organisations. There need be no contradiction between freedom of information and protection of privacy.

As far as Ministers and civil servants are concerned, the most contentious area is that of advice, opinion or recommendation for the purposes of policy-making. Anti-secrecy campaigners tend to be divided over this.

The journalist David Leigh, in his book *The Frontiers of Secrecy*, argues as follows:

> Civil servants would like to claim wide exemptions for 'policy advice'. This must be resisted. If officials are trying to persuade a Minister, for example, to increase maximum lorry weights or to build nuclear power stations, then the public should know that that is the attitude of the department. There may be a case for protecting minutes of internal meetings in a department, and minutes of Cabinet and Cabinet Committee meetings. There is not a good case, but only a mythological one, for protecting deliberate and considered options put before Ministers, or before Cabinets and their committees – or comments and pressures on a department from outside lobbyists and from other departments.

In the book mentioned several times before, *The Civil Service*, Peter Kellner and Lord Crowther-Hunt say:

> The unspoken heart of the argument for closed government is that private debate among civil servants and Ministers produces more *rational* policies, free from public pressure, which is assumed to be irrational. Wise men, cogitating quietly on the nation's problems, will produce 'right' answers if they are sheltered from the hubbub of the political market place, but once exposed to pressure groups and vested interests and newspapers that will get it all wrong, who knows what absurdities will result?

Various secondary arguments are deployed to make an essential contempt for democratic debate more palatable.

They say that 'the central argument of most civil servants and Ministers, however, does not concern the sensible exceptions. It concerns the character of policy-making, of government administration, and of democratic debate. The essence . . . is that they provide little if any evidence for this hypothesis. On the contrary, a number of instances of closed government that have come to light suggest that it can actually encourage bad policy making and bad administration.' They then cite the decision to build *Concorde*, the breaking of oil sanctions on Rhodesia, the deferment of child benefits, education policy, and charity status for public schools. They conclude: 'In each case the decisions that were taken reflected not so much wise, rational men arriving at considered judgements, as ordinary frail mortals using closed government to hide their inadequacies.'

The civil service arguments

The former Head of the Civil Service, Lord Croham, discussing this matter in 1979, stated:

> The early release of these documents (assessments and decisions made by named officials) could be expected to lead to a degree of open comment about the performance and judgement of those individuals and inferences being made (almost certainly wrongly) about their political views. There are many who think that this openness would be a good thing – it could lead – although I think it unlikely – in the direction of a much less anonymous civil service actively engaged in open argument and vigorously defending itself, not only without the help of Ministers, but even against Ministers – a situation which I think would have many undesirable consequences. It is far more likely in this country to lead to a much greater reluctance to give firm advice in writing and/or to express individual options on record. The chances are that this would lead to an unwillingness to delegate authority or to accept delegation – with a constant need to refer upwards, slowing down the process of decision-making. It could be that it would also lead to an over-rigid reliance on precedence and a reduction in the extent of discretion.

Senior civil servants advance two reasons why their policy advice should remain secret. The first is that whereas Ministers are vulnerable to the democratic process, civil servants continue in office serving one party in power after another, one Minister after another, and if the policies of successive administrations differ widely, then they have to pursue first one set of policies and then another, always appearing to be devoted to the wishes of their political masters. It is a rather extraordinary position, and in order that it can be maintained with any dignity, it is necessary for any record of advice they may have given to earlier Ministers to be kept secret. Thus, a Minister cannot, when assuming office, see the files of his predecessor.

The fact is, of course, that most civil servants *do* hold opinions on most subjects, and thus the secrecy is employed to cover up that reality. In effect, it preserves a lie – that civil servants are impartial between one approach and another. It is doubtful whether the public interest is well-served by the perpetuation of that lie. Given the enormous power that civil servants have to prejudice decision-making in support of their own views, there is a case for making them more publicly accountable.

The second point that civil servants would make is as follows: In the process of policy-making, there has to be a free and frank exchange of views; ideas have to be tested, factors have to be balanced honestly and without concern about misunderstanding by those who are not present and are just reading the record . . . In the process of testing ideas, people must be able to expose themselves to being proven wrong without loss of credibility . . . and so on . . . and so on.

I do not entirely share the points of view of either David Leigh or Kellner and Crowther-Hunt on this latter point. I believe that there is some substance in this argument. In the planning of organisations I have been involved in, there has always been a stage when it has been necessary to argue out the options freely and frankly and in privacy. Indeed, even in the planning of the 1984 Campaign for Freedom of Information we had our free and frank exchanges of views about our policy. Those discussions took place in private and were the better for it. We were able to speak more honestly, test our theories, learn together, and this was an entirely healthy process. We needed to produce certain documents on which to base these discussions – documents that could be tossed away after they served their purpose. We were forced to ask ourselves, at the end of this process, whether we should deny Ministers and senior civil servants the same advantages that we had obtained for ourselves from confidential expression of opinion.

The problem in drafting FoI legislation is to allow such exchanges on paper and in private whilst at the same time encouraging the availability of far more of the background information, and of the main options, and the factors supporting one or another. Not only is it of importance that as much information as possible be published, but it should be published *during the process of policy-making*, and not merely to explain why a particular decision has been taken. There has to be the maximum opportunity for the maximum number of people to be involved in policy-making, to challenge orthodox thinking, to propose particular options, and this is only possible where outsiders have access to the facts and figures and other information available to the decision-makers.

On most issues, policy-making includes a number of phases: background research, accumulation of the opinions of interested parties, the production of options with costings and potential benefits . . . There is no reason why all these should not be open. Only in the latter st civil servants and Ministers have to extend beyond the facts tc judgements, including the political implications for the government, and implications with respect to its wider strategy. It is in the closing stages where civil servants may sum up the political options for Ministers, or strategic considerations, that their documents could justifiably be considered confidential.

In fact, there is not that much of a contradiction between what I argue and what was recommended by the Croham Directive and what has been discussed when voluntary measures have been proposed before – namely, that the background information should be published and only the recommendations kept confidential. However, there are three substantial differences. First, I would seek the maximum publication of information *during* policy-making to improve participation; second, the voluntary approach would be replaced by legislation; third, that legislation would have to be sufficiently tightly drafted to guarantee that exempted papers or recommendations did not incorporate information that should be freely available. This will not be easy.

The problem with stating that even the political and strategic recommendations of Ministers should be available is that much advice would not be put on paper at all, but merely conveyed in conversation and unrecorded meetings, and, second, if advice is recorded, that it would become more cautious and more calculated to protect the advice-giver than serve the public interest.

If it is unrealistic to pretend that one can end the confidentiality of political and strategic advice by civil servants to Ministers, it is better to acknowledge that it exists and concentrate on creating ways of ensuring that the major intention of FoI legislation – to make the same facts and figures and arguments available to the public as are available to Ministers – is in fact achieved. In my view this concession to reality is also likely to encourage greater support for FoI legislation from civil servants.

Civil servants should be warned, however, that legislation can after a suitable period be amended and improved, and the misuse of an exemption to continue to keep secret facts as well as opinion could lead to tougher legislation in the longer term.

Ministerial accountability

The exemptions I have outlined deal with one of the main contentions of the defenders of secrecy: namely, that an element of secrecy is necessary. That much is conceded and it is accommodated – it is in no way inconsistent with legislation that creates and institutionalises a presumption that information should be available unless there is an established reason for withholding it.

Before moving to the positive question of freedom of information legislation, let's look at the other main argument of its opponents, namely, that while it may work in countries like the United States, it is not consistent with the operation of a Westminster-style democracy, and in particular with ministerial accountability.

The fact is that Ministers cannot genuinely be responsible for, and knowledgeable about all that happens within their Ministries. 'It is a fiction', wrote James Cornford in 1978, 'with real political consequences, since civil servants must live in fear of embarrassing Ministers and Ministers must defend actions of which they neither knew nor approved, and which may, indeed, have been taken when they were not even in charge. Freedom of information would certainly threaten this fiction. That is no reason for denying information, but an accurate reason for finding more sensible ways of controlling administration.'

The Senate Standing Committee on Constitutional and Legal Affairs on the Freedom of Information Bill 1978 in Australia, confronted this issue directly:

> Many of those who do not share our enthusiasm for freedom of information, or for opening the processes of government to greater public scrutiny, frequently take refuge in saying that such concepts are somehow incompatible with a system of government based, as ours is, upon the Westminster model . . . We reject such arguments and assert strongly that there is nothing in the Westminster system which should operate to preclude Australia from having an effective FoI Bill. As we shall show, opponents of the Bill have frequently misunderstood what the Westminster system is, or else have misrepresented how it actually operates in our contemporary society. We conclude that an effective Freedom of Information Bill, far from being incompatible with the Westminster system, may in fact have the potential to strengthen it.

> The characteristic features of a Westminster system are usually stated to be:

> (a) that the *Executive is to be found as part of and not as separate from the Legislature;* that is, that ministers are all members of the Parliament;

> (b) that there is a doctrine and practice of *collective ministerial responsibility* usually expressed in the phrase 'Cabinet solidarity' which requires all ministers to consider themselves equally responsible for and bound by the decisions of the executive government;

> (c) that there is a doctrine of *individual ministerial responsibility* which holds that each minister is personally responsible for all of the decisions made and carried out by the department which he heads;

> (d) that the government of the day is served by a *public service which remains politically neutral and in no way involved in partisan controversies* so that it is able to serve any government regardless of its political complexion with an equal degree of loyalty and efficiency;

> (e) that *the members of the public service remain as far as possible personally anonymous,* so that particular views are not ascribed to individual public servants, and so that the views of public servants are not seen to be at variance with the views ultimately expressed by the executive government.

The report concluded:

> We are firmly of the opinion that, while the changes which we recommend will have the effect of exposing somewhat more of the operation of government in Australia, they will in no way derogate from the principle of collective ministerial responsibility, a principle which we regard as vital . . . and which we would in no way seek to weaken. Indeed, it will be seen that our recommendations, if adopted, would clearly protect the confidentiality of all Cabinet deliberations; they would preserve the necessary degree of secrecy for advice tended to Cabinet and would in no way expose the individual views or opinions of ministers in a way which could adversely affect the doctrine of collective responsibility.

The report then discussed the shift of real power from the elected politicians to the public service, which it acknowledged existed in Australia as well as in Britain, and stated:

> This shift in the balance of power and the elected government and the professional public service has important implications for freedom of information legislation. In essence it means that the public service should be made more open to public scrutiny and more accountable for its actions than has traditionally been the case. We do not believe that this changed attitude is in any way incompatible with the principles of the Westminster system.

On the question of neutrality of the public service, the Australian report (which incidentally is far more substantial than any report produced in Britain on freedom of information) states that the publication of advice by civil servants would end 'the specious or expedient advice, the unsubstantiated comments about individuals, or the expression of mere opinions without any real support'. It quoted the Fulton Committee in Britain as saying:

> We think that administration suffers from the conviction, which is still alive in many fields, that only the Minister should explain issues in public and what his department is or is not doing about them . . . In our view, therefore, the convention of anonymity should be modified and civil servants, as professional administrators, should be able to go further than now in explaining what their departments are doing, at any rate, so far as concerns managing existing policies and implementing legislation.

The report completes its examination of this subject with these words:

> We value the Westminster system of government; we do not seek to change it; nor do we believe effective freedom of information legislation would change it. A great deal of the talk about the Westminster system and how it would be altered by freedom of information legislation has been obscure and misleading. To a great extent the term 'Westminster system' has been used as a smoke-screen behind which to hide, and with which to cover up existing practices of

unnecessary secrecy. Very often people have alleged that the Westminster system is under attack by freedom of information legislation when what is actually under attack is their own traditional and convenient way of doing things, immune from public gaze and scrutiny. We are indeed seeking to put an end to that. What matters is not the convenience of ministers or public servants, but what contributes to better government. The only feature of the Westminster system which cannot be in any way modified without fundamentally subverting that system is the need to ensure that members of the Executive Government are part of, and drawn from, the Legislature. Freedom of information legislation does not alter this one iota. The other features of the Westminster system which we have identified will either not be significantly changed by our freedom of information proposals or else will, we believe, be changed for the better.

Freedom of information legislation does not relate to any specific system of government, be it a Westminster, presidential or any other system. It is rather a question of attitudes, a view about the nature of government, how it works and what its relationship is to the people it is supposed to be serving. Any political system which holds that the people are entitled to a maximum degree of information about how *their* government operates, so that it can be made more responsive and accountable to them, will welcome an effective Freedom of Information Bill. In this respect a Westminster system of government should be no different from any other.

I have quoted mainly the conclusions of that Senate Standing Committee, but they are backed up by pages of argument and evidence and represent the best discussion of the issue available in print.

FoI legislation and its objectives

Mrs Thatcher has also expressed the fear that the final decisions will be removed from the elected assembly and taken to the courts, thus removing a key aspect of power from the legislature to the judiciary. If this is a widely shared concern, it is possible to introduce freedom of information legislation, with the final court of appeal being a Special Tribunal (possibly of MPs). Of course it can be argued that as citizens are ultimately answerable to the courts for their respect for a thousand and one laws, rules and regulations, there is no reason why government should not be equally responsible to the courts for respecting the law. Nevertheless, the draft Act the Campaign has circulated provides for an Information Commissioner who will be the first court of appeal on the working of the Act, with the right of further appeal to a Freedom of Information Tribunal if either the statutory authority or the individual remain dissatisfied.

There should be a number of objectives of FoI legislation:

● It should institutionalise a presumption that all administration should be open, except where there are clearly-defined overriding reasons for secrecy.

● It should firmly commit politicians and civil servants to implement the principles in practice.

- It should remove all unjustified barriers to the implementation of the spirit of the legislation.

- It should set up the mechanisms whereby this can be achieved.

The machinery of administration should also meet a number of requirements:

- It should ensure publicity of what information exists.

- It should establish a way whereby the public can obtain that information easily and quickly.

- It should create an opportunity for appeal where the information is denied.

- It should enable the monitoring and reviewing of the legislation.

- It should define the exemptions and guarantee that information is properly protected.

Thus, the proposal for Britain is as follows:

First, parliament should repeal the Official Secrets Act. It should replace it with narrow provisions concerned only with national security, and as tightly drawn as possible.

Parliament should then pass a Freedom of Information Act, creating a public right of access to official information, and place upon the information-holders an obligation to disclose. This should not only cover Whitehall, but also local authorities, and other statutory bodies. It should place upon organisations in the private sector a statutory obligation to give access to, and disclose, such information as may be required by the public interest.

Either this Act, or supplementary Acts, should deal with open administration, i.e. public access to meetings, etc. Either this Act or a supplementary Act should create the right of individuals to have access to their own files.

The Act should specify the time period within which the information-holders must respond. The Act must contain appeal and enforcement procedures. The Campaign for Freedom of Information has drafted a Bill to incorporate all of these proposals and it was introduced under the Ten Minute Rule Bill by David Steel. It remains, however, very much a 'discussion document' and is being widely circulated for further fine-tuning.

(In the spring of 1984 the Campaign, thinking that this might not be the appropriate time politically to seek to push a full Freedom of Information Act through the House of Commons, was considering a number of narrower Acts – an Access to Personal Files Act, an Environmental Information Act, and a Local Government (Access to Information) Act and an Act to withdraw the option from water authorities to act in secret. These have all been drafted and await the appropriate opportunity for further promotion in the House.)

The future

I have no doubt that this legislation will one day be introduced and one day be passed. I believe that one day, after these reforms are implemented, men and women will marvel at the way we had allowed information in Britain to be so restricted. They will marvel that people could not see their own files and had no opportunity to check, correct, or appeal the details. They will marvel at the number of local issues allowed to be discussed behind closed doors by local authorities. They will not know whether to laugh or cry at the obsession with secrecy in Whitehall and the classification of the most harmless information as confidential. They will see how secrecy allowed incompetence and corruption to remain unchecked; how secrecy was employed to load the dice in support of the status quo, to preserve power and position, and to protect from embarrassment. And they will chuckle at the weakness of the defence for it and be astonished at how all attempts to crack the safe of official secrecy repeatedly failed.

I believe too that history will show that the introduction of FoI legislation in Britain led not to more inefficiency but to less; saved much more money than it cost; created greater understanding between people and their administrators than before; improved the quality of public participation and reduced not just the concentration of power but the strain of responsibility on governing institutions; that it created a greater sense of security and improved public health and safety; that it created greater faith in the justice of our law and institutions – that it engendered greater trust at all levels of society.

I believe the kind of legislation I have described, particularly when it is reflected in its spirit as well as in its detail, will make Britain a better, fairer, more democratic place.

FURTHER INFORMATION

Books

Books referred to on earlier pages, all of them worthwhile further reading, include:

The Franks Report, Dept. Committee on Section 2 of the Official Secrets Act 1911, September 1972, Cmnd 5104 HMSO.

The Civil Service: Report of the Fulton Committee, 1968, Cmnd 638 HMSO.

Report of the Committee on Data Protection, 1978, Cmnd 7341 HMSO.

The Civil Servants: An Inquiry into Britain's Ruling Class, Peter Kellner and Lord Crowther-Hunt, MacDonald 1980.

The Frontiers of Secrecy: Closed Government in Britain, David Leigh, Junction Books 1980.

The Politics of Secrecy, James Michael, Penguin 1982.

Consuming Secrets: A Report for the National Consumer Council, edited by Rosemary Delbridge and Martin Smith, Burnett Books 1982.

Your Disobedient Servant, Leslie Chapman, Penguin 1979.

Tenth Report of the Royal Commission on Environmental Pollution.

The Campaign for Freedom of Information

The Campaign for Freedom of Information's address is 2 Northdown Street, London N1 9BG. Tel: 01-278 9686.

INDEX